THE MORMON TRAIL
AND THE
LATTER-DAY SAINTS
IN AMERICAN HISTORY

Other titles *in American History*

IN
★AMERICAN★
HISTORY

THE MORMON TRAIL
AND THE
LATTER-DAY SAINTS
IN AMERICAN HISTORY

Carol Rust Nash

Enslow Publishers, Inc.

44 Fadem Road   PO Box 38
Box 699   Aldershot
Springfield, NJ 07081   Hants GU12 6BP
USA   UK

http://www.enslow.com

This book is dedicated to my family and friends in Utah,
Mormons and non-Mormons.

Library of Congress Cataloging-in-Publication Data

Nash, Carol Rust.
    The Mormon trail and the Latter-day Saints in American history/ Carol
Rust Nash.
        p. cm. — (In American history)
    Includes bibliographical references and index.
    Summary: Explores the founding of the Latter-day Saints by Joseph
Smith, their persecution, the migration west led by Brigham Young, the
church's legacy, and its present role in society.
    ISBN 0-89490-988-6
    1. Church of Jesus Christ of Latter-day Saints—History—Juvenile
literature. 2. Mormon Church—United States—History—Juvenile
literature. 3. Mormon Trail—Juvenile literature. [1. Church of Jesus
Christ of Latter-day Saints. 2. Mormon Church. 3. Mormon Trail.]
I. Title. II. Series.
BX8611.N37 1999
289.3'73—DC21   98-35588
                                                                     CIP
                                                                     AC

Printed in the United States of America

10 9 8 7 6 5 4 3 2 1

To Our Readers:
All Internet addresses in this book were active and appropriate when we
went to press. Any comments or suggestions can be sent by e-mail to
Comments@enslow.com or to the address on the back cover.

Illustration Credits: *American Advertising Posters of the Nineteenth
Century from the Bella C. Landauer Collection of the New-York Historical
Society,* Published by Dover Publications, Inc., in 1976, p. 106; Carol
Rust Nash, pp. 89, 113; Enslow Publishers, Inc., p. 81; LDS Historical
Department Archives, pp. 10, 15, 21, 28, 37, 47, 51, 58, 64, 70, 79, 87,
88; Reproduced from the *Dictionary of American Portraits,* Published by
Dover Publications, Inc., in 1967, pp. 9, 20, 25, 60, 61, 74, 77, 85, 96.

Cover Illustration: Carol Rust Nash; LDS Historical Department
Archives; Reproduced from the *Dictionary of American Portraits,*
Published by Dover Publications, Inc., in 1967.

★ CONTENTS ★

★ ACKNOWLEDGMENT ★

Special thanks go to Deborah McKown, my friend and copyeditor.

The Church of Jesus Christ of Latter-day Saints is a worldwide organization with 10 million members. The only major religion to have its roots in the United States, it now has more members outside the country than inside. Though the majority of Latter-day Saints reside in the Western Hemisphere, members live in more than 160 countries, and the church has more than 50 temples around the world.

THE VISION OF A TEENAGE BOY

It all began in 1820 with the prayer of a fourteen-year-old boy in a grove of trees behind his father's log house. That boy, Joseph Smith, Jr., founded a church whose followers were instrumental in the settlement of the American West.

Where It Began

They were seekers, healers, and visionaries. Some screamed and cried. Some rolled on the floor. Others walked on all fours and barked like dogs, and some spoke in unintelligible languages. Some jerked, head and limbs thrashing back and forth, distorting their bodies. They were all caught up in the Second Great

Awakening, a religious revival that began in Connecticut in 1797 and continued until the early 1830s.

New religions sprouted all through the towns and countryside. The religious outburst, with its warnings of hell, fire, and damnation, swept through western New York with such enthusiasm that the area was referred to as the "burned-over district."

This was the atmosphere that surrounded fourteen-year-old Joseph Smith, Jr. Confused by the issue of which church to join, he walked to a grove outside his home in Palmyra, New York, where he knelt in prayer and asked for God's help. Smith said God the Father and his son, Jesus Christ, appeared to him and told him that none of the existing churches was true; he should join none of them.

Joseph Smith's Destiny

After his first vision in 1820, Joseph Smith worked for a while as a treasure seeker. Hunting for buried treasure in New England was not uncommon during the early nineteenth century. Smith later referred to treasure-seeking as one of the "vices and follies" of youthful indiscretion.[1]

In 1823, when Smith was seventeen, he said an angel had appeared to him while he was praying in his room. The angel told him about hidden golden plates that contained a history of the original people on the North American continent during the time of Christ. The angel, whom Smith said called himself Moroni, told him where the plates were buried and instructed him to share the story of the visitation with his father. Smith said the angel appeared twice more that night, repeating the same message each time.

The next day, as Smith worked in the fields with his father and brother Alvin, he thought about telling his father about the angel's visit but feared his father would not believe him. Feeling ill, Smith left the fields for home, and the angel again came to him. Smith said the angel assured him that his father would "believe every word. . . ."[2]

Smith went back to the field, found his father, and told him the story. His father not only believed him, but told him the visions were from God. Smith then left to find the place where the angel had said the plates were buried.

As a young man, Joseph Smith said he had a series of visions that later led to the formation of the Church of Jesus Christ of Latter-day Saints.

Smith went to the west slope of a hill called Cumorah. Using a stick as a lever, he moved a stone and uncovered a box. When Smith removed the box and opened it, he found inside golden plates engraved with symbols. He also found an instrument called the Urim and Thummim, which was used by ancient seers to aid in the translation of spiritual messages. The instrument was a pair of translucent stones set in silver bows, like eyeglasses, and attached to a breastplate such as a warrior might wear.

It was at a hill called Cumorah that Joseph Smith said he found the golden plates of which the angel had spoken.

The angel then appeared again and told Smith it was not the time for the plates to be taken. Smith said the angel instructed him to return in one year.

That evening, Joseph Smith shared his experience with his family. They believed his tale and were excited. But as the news of his experience filtered out into the community, many, especially the preachers, rejected the story. Leaders of the most popular sects in the area called Smith a liar and a faker.

One year later, in September 1824, Joseph Smith, now eighteen, returned to that spot on Cumorah to retrieve the plates. However, when he attempted to remove them, he was struck by a force that knocked him onto his back. The angel Moroni appeared and told him to return again in one year.

Smith returned to the site in 1825 and again in 1826, but both times the angel Moroni turned him away. According to Smith, he was eventually allowed to remove the golden plates, which led to the formation of a whole new religion.

2

A CHURCH IS FORMED

Joseph Smith was born on December 23, 1805, in the town of Sharon, Vermont, the fourth child of Lucy Mack and Joseph Smith, Sr. The family moved to Lebanon, New Hampshire, when Joseph was five years old and to Palmyra, New York, when he was ten. A poor but hardworking family, they had been unlucky in matters of finance and had been swindled out of what resources they had in a bad business deal, according to Joseph's mother.[1]

The family supported itself by hiring out for day labor and running a small shop that sold gingerbread, boiled eggs, and root beer. The father and the older sons reportedly also brought in some money by digging for buried treasure with the help of a seer stone. These stones, often natural crystals, were supposed to give certain individuals the ability to "see" invisible things and to tell the future.

The Smiths acquired enough money to purchase a hundred acres of land in Manchester Township, south of Palmyra. They built a log house and began the task of clearing the heavily wooded land.

Joseph could read and write but had little formal

education. Both of his parents had occasionally taught school, so he received most of his education at home. He was outgoing, cheerful, full of imagination, and "born to leadership, but hampered by meager education and grinding poverty."[2]

Treasure Seeker

In October 1825, Joseph Smith was hired by Josiah Stowel to search for a silver mine in the Susquehanna River valley that was rumored to have been worked by the Spanish.[3] Smith's mother wrote that Stowel had come from Pennsylvania to see her son "on account of having heard that he possessed certain keys, by which he could discern things invisible to the natural eye."[4]

Before Smith had been allowed to take the golden plates, he had found a seer stone while digging a well. He would place the stone inside a hat, put his face into the hat, and "see" where to dig for buried treasure. This practice was not new. Many references to "gazing" are found in history. Egyptians gazed into a pool of ink. Greeks used a mirror. Aztecs stared into a quartz crystal. Europeans stared at a sword blade or into a glass of wine or sherry. "Seers" used any translucent or reflective surface that causes the eyes to blur after long periods of staring at it.

While working for Stowel, Smith stayed at the home of Isaac Hale, a famous hunter. It was there, on the banks of the Susquehanna River in Harmony, Pennsylvania, that twenty-year-old Smith met Hale's daughter, Emma. She was a dark, serious-faced woman with luminous hazel eyes. One year older than Smith, she was quiet, with an unapproachable air that Smith, already described as a "great favorite with the ladies," found attractive.[5]

Smith was by now a big, powerful man, but he walked with a slight limp due to an infection he had when he was eight years old. The limp, however, did not detract from his appearance. He was described as handsome, in spite of his prominent, curved nose. He had large blue eyes and long lashes that immediately drew attention to his face.

Legal Troubles

Smith's treasure-seeking brought about the beginning of legal troubles that would plague him throughout his life. He was summoned to court on March 20, 1826. Smith was charged with disorderly conduct and with being an impostor by Peter G. Bridgman, one of Josiah Stowel's neighbors. The court found Smith guilty, but the record does not say what sentence was passed.

Emma and Joseph Smith

Smith lived with Josiah Stowel after the trial. He did not want to return to Palmyra without Emma, with whom he had fallen in love, but he was no longer welcome at Isaac Hale's home. Because of Smith's legal troubles and treasure-seeking activities, Hale had refused Smith's request to marry Emma and had driven Smith from his property. Smith and Emma would

Joseph Smith fell in love with Emma Hale, despite the disapproval of her father, and encouraged her to run off with him.

meet secretly, however, when Hale was away on hunting trips. Smith begged her to run away with him.

Stowel was fond of the couple and arranged a rendezvous for them at his home in South Bainbridge. From there, they went to the home of Squire Tarbell, a justice of the peace, and were married on January 18, 1827. The couple then headed north to live with Smith's parents in Manchester.

In August, eight months after the wedding, they went to Harmony to get Emma's things and to face her father for the first time since their marriage.

Smith did not have a wagon, so he hired Peter Ingersoll, a neighbor, to take them to the northern Pennsylvania town. Ingersoll said their arrival at Hale's house was a "truly affecting" scene. He said Hale spoke "in a flood of tears" and accused Smith of stealing his daughter.[6] Hale told Smith that he would rather have seen her dead than married to someone who spent all his time digging for money, pretending to see into a stone, and deceiving people. Hale then told Smith that if he would be willing to work for a living and move to Pennsylvania, he would assist Smith in getting into a business. According to Ingersoll, Smith agreed, and Ingersoll, Smith, and Emma returned to Manchester.

Golden Plates

On his fifth annual trip to the hill called Cumorah, on September 22, 1827, twenty-one-year-old Joseph Smith said he was finally allowed to remove the golden plates and the Urim and Thummim from the box and take them home to translate.

According to Smith, the plates were about the size of book pages—eight inches square—and no thicker than sheet metal. Made of pure gold, they were bound with three huge wire rings. The plates were engraved with characters that Smith later referred to as reformed Egyptian, the Nephite language. According to the Book of Mormon, the Nephites and the Lamanites were early inhabitants of the North American continent and ancestors of the American Indians.

Members of the Church of Jesus Christ of Latter-day Saints believe the book is an account of the Nephites and Lamanites, edited by the prophet Mormon, along with his son, Moroni (the angel who appeared to Smith), who was the last of a long line of historians. Mormon and Moroni, along with others who preceded them, recorded their story on the golden plates that had been given to Smith to translate.

The book tells how Lehi—a descendant of Joseph, who was sold into slavery in Egypt by his brothers—his wife, Sariah, and his four sons (Laman, Lemuel, Sam, and Nephi) left Jerusalem and sailed to the Western Hemisphere. Lehi's descendants split into two groups, the Nephites and the Lamanites. According to the Book of Mormon, the Lamanites destroyed the Nephites about two hundred years after Jesus Christ visited the North American continent immediately following his resurrection. Members of the Church of

SOURCE DOCUMENT

1. AND NOW I, MORMON, BEING ABOUT TO DELIVER UP THE RECORD WHICH I HAVE BEEN MAKING INTO THE HANDS OF MY SON MORONI, BEHOLD I HAVE WITNESSED ALMOST ALL THE DESTRUCTION OF MY PEOPLE, THE NEPHITES. . . .

4. AND THE THINGS WHICH ARE UPON THESE PLATES PLEASING ME, BECAUSE OF THE PROPHESIES OF THE COMING OF CHRIST; AND MY FATHERS KNOWING THAT MANY OF THEM HAVE BEEN FULFILLED; YEA, AND I ALSO KNOW THAT AS MANY THINGS AS HAVE BEEN PROPHESIED CONCERNING IT DOWN TO THIS DAY HAVE BEEN FULFILLED, AND AS MANY AS GO BEYOND THIS DAY MUST SURELY COME TO PASS—[7]

The Book of Mormon, according to Joseph Smith, contained an account of the history of Jesus Christ's visit to North America, as recorded by several ancient historians, including Mormon and his son, Moroni.

Jesus Christ of Latter-day Saints believe that some of the American Indians are descendants of Laman.

When Smith removed the plates, he said the angel warned him not to show them to anyone. Smith showed his mother the Urim and Thummim but warned her and the rest of the family that they could not look at the golden plates.

Smith frequently changed the hiding place of the plates as word spread that he possessed a treasure. Because of constant interruptions from his family and neighbors, Smith found it impossible to tackle the job of translating the plates. In December 1827, he and Emma moved back to Harmony into a house owned by her father.

Martin Harris, a prosperous farmer who believed Smith's claim that the golden plates were of divine origin, financed their trip. He agreed to join Smith later and help in the process of translation by taking dictation. Smith would read the inscriptions on the plates, and Harris would write down what he said.

Translation Begins

In order to translate the plates, Joseph and Emma Smith worked together. They divided a room by stringing up a rope and draping a blanket across it so Emma could not see the plates. They worked through the makeshift barrier, with Joseph Smith on one side reading the plates and Emma on the other side, taking dictation.

Although Emma never saw the plates, she claimed to have felt them once when she was dusting and moved them as they lay wrapped in a linen tablecloth.[8]

When Martin Harris arrived at Smith's home in April 1828 to check on the book's progress and to help, he found the couple desperately poor and Emma pregnant. On June 15, the Smiths' first child, Alvin, was born, but the infant died the same day.

Translation Completed

David Whitmer was a young farmer from Fayette, New York, and a friend of Oliver Cowdery, a young schoolteacher who replaced Martin Harris as scribe. Cowdery was more efficient at taking dictation than Harris was. At one point, Smith allowed Whitmer to observe the process of translation. After hearing about the project, David's father, Peter Whitmer, Sr., offered free room and board to Smith and Cowdery in Fayette while they finished the work.

Harris waited around the Whitmer house for the book's completion because Smith had told him early in the translation process that three witnesses would be allowed to see the plates. In June 1829, Smith said that Harris, Cowdery, and David Whitmer would be the witnesses. The four men walked into the woods and knelt in prayer. According to the testimony of the men, the angel Moroni appeared to them, showed them the Urim and Thummim and the golden plates, "and commanded them to bear witness of

David Whitmer, a farmer who learned of Joseph Smith's attempts to translate the golden plates, became one of the church's early members, as well as one of the three witnesses allowed to see the plates.

their existence to the world."[9] Smith later showed the plates to eight other witnesses. After displaying the plates, Smith said he gave the plates and the Urim and Thummim back to Moroni.

The translation was completed in July 1829, and with Harris's financial help, the printing of the Book of Mormon began. Harris had agreed to mortgage his farm if necessary to guarantee the $3,000 needed to print the books. He ended up selling his farm to meet the costs of printing and binding five thousand copies. On March 26, 1830, the Book of Mormon went on sale in a Palmyra bookstore. The testimony of the eleven witnesses was printed on the flyleaf (a blank page at the beginning or end of a book) of the first edition and has been printed in all editions since.

These are the three witnesses—Martin Harris, David Whitmer, and Oliver Cowdery, clockwise from bottom right—who were permitted by Smith to see the golden plates.

SOURCE DOCUMENT

BE IT KNOWN UNTO ALL NATIONS, KINDREDS, TONGUES, AND PEOPLE, UNTO WHOM THIS WORK SHALL COME: THAT WE, THROUGH THE GRACE OF GOD THE FATHER, AND OUR LORD JESUS CHRIST, HAVE SEEN THE PLATES WHICH CONTAIN THIS RECORD, WHICH IS A RECORD OF THE PEOPLE OF NEPHI, AND ALSO OF THE LAMANITES. . . . AND WE ALSO KNOW THAT THEY HAVE BEEN TRANSLATED BY THE GIFT AND POWER OF GOD, FOR HIS VOICE HATH DECLARED IT UNTO US; WHEREFORE WE KNOW OF A SURETY THAT THE WORK IS TRUE. AND WE ALSO TESTIFY THAT WE HAVE SEEN THE ENGRAVINGS WHICH ARE UPON THE PLATES; AND THEY HAVE BEEN SHOWN UNTO US BY THE POWER OF GOD, AND NOT OF MAN. . . .

OLIVER COWDERY
DAVID WHITMER
MARTIN HARRIS[10]

The testimony of the three first witnesses and the eight later witnesses, who had seen the golden plates, has appeared in every edition that has ever been printed of the Book of Mormon.

New Church Is Formed

The Church of Christ was officially organized on April 6, 1830, in the home of Peter Whitmer, Sr., in Fayette, New York. Joseph Smith served the sacrament (communion). Mormonism had begun.

Three years later, the Church of Christ was renamed the Church of Latter-day Saints. In 1838, the name was changed again to the Church of Jesus Christ of Latter-day Saints—the name it uses today. The church is often referred to by its nicknames, the LDS Church or the Mormon Church. Its members are sometimes called Mormons. The term "Mormon" was used in contempt in the early years, but it does not carry that connotation today.

The church grew quickly. Within a month, membership had jumped to forty, and many baptisms were performed as the story of Smith and the golden plates spread. But for each person Smith baptized, several others thought him a fraud and a blasphemer.

A group of nonbelievers destroyed a dam that Smith's followers had constructed across a stream to make a pool for baptisms. After it was rebuilt, a mob of about fifty men surrounded a house where Smith and his converts were meeting and trapped them inside. That night, a constable came to the door with a warrant for Smith's arrest. The charge was one familiar to Smith—disorderly conduct.

Smith declared his innocence, and the constable confessed that the warrant had been a ploy to get Joseph Smith into the hands of the mob. He had to take Smith to court, but he promised he would keep him from a tar-and-feather party (covering a person with hot, melted tar and feathers). The horses galloped under the constable's whip all the way to South Bainbridge as Smith was carried to safety.

After an all-day session, the court acquitted Smith of the charge. The moment the verdict was read, however, another constable seized Smith, served him with yet another warrant for disorderly conduct, and took him to a neighboring county for trial. The quality of Smith's character was debated until two o'clock in the morning, when he was again acquitted.

While the harassment of Smith continued in Fayette, misfortune befell the rest of the Smith family in Palmyra. Creditors got warrants for the arrest of Smith's older brother Hyrum and his father for outstanding debts. Hyrum fled for Colesville before the constable arrived. Joseph Smith, Sr., was taken to jail.

Joseph and Emma Smith, concerned about the family's financial troubles and the hostility Smith was encountering in western New York, decided to return to Emma's father's farm in Harmony, where they could live quietly.

After a short time, Cowdery became impatient with Smith's absence. He visited Smith and urged him to get back to church business. Not long after this visit, Emma and Smith moved back to the Whitmer home in Fayette. Emma never saw her parents again.

Missionaries

Smith sent his brother Samuel to southern New York to spread word of the new church, and he sent Cowdery to the east. Thus began a formal missionary system that remains an important part of the church today.

Late in the summer of 1830, Smith called Cowdery back and asked him to go west to convert the American Indians and to scout the area for a spot where they could take the converts and build a city of Zion—a place where they could live and worship without harassment.

Cowdery enlisted a new convert for his mission. Parley Pratt had come from Ohio to New York to preach and had been converted by Smith's brother Hyrum. A member of the church for only three weeks, Pratt headed west with Cowdery and two other men to baptize new members.

Pratt convinced Cowdery's party to stop in Mentor, Ohio, to visit Sidney Rigdon, a famous orator. Less than three weeks after the missionary party had arrived, Rigdon and his community of about one hundred people were baptized into Joseph Smith's new church.

Orator Sidney Rigdon converted to the church in 1830 and quickly became Joseph Smith's good friend and counselor.

Rigdon, then in his late thirties, set off immediately for New York to meet Smith, accompanied by Edward Partridge, a prosperous Kirtland hatter. Smith and Rigdon quickly became friends, and Rigdon became Smith's counselor, a leadership position in the church.

While Rigdon was in New York, Smith reported a revelation that instructed him to relocate the church to Kirtland, Ohio. Plans were made for the sixty-member congregation to move.

In January 1831, Smith and Emma, who was pregnant for the second time, climbed into a sleigh with Rigdon and Partridge and began the three-hundred-mile trip west.

John Wentworth, the editor of the *Chicago Democrat*, requested a history of the Church of Jesus Christ of Latter-day Saints in the spring of 1842. In his response, Joseph Smith included statements of the Mormons' beliefs, which were later known as the Articles of Faith. These were not a complete list of beliefs, but a summary of the church's position on contemporary religious issues. Some of the beliefs listed in the Articles of Faith are:

LATTER-DAY SAINTS' BELIEFS

- God the Father; His son, Jesus Christ; and the Holy Ghost exist as three separate personages.
- Jesus Christ will again reign on the earth.
- People will be punished for their sins.
- All people may be saved by obeying the laws of the gospel.
- Repentance and baptism are the first principles of the church.
- The Bible is the word of God, as far as it is translated correctly, and the Book of Mormon is also the word of God.

- People should be allowed to worship God in their own way.
- Laws of the government should be obeyed.[1]

As the years passed, Smith reported new revelations, which created doctrines that are different from many Christian religions.

One of these doctrines is the belief that God was once a human being, and that all people, if they live righteous lives, can become gods. Many non-Mormons saw this relationship with God and the concept of multiple gods as blasphemy.

Another belief, unusual to the Mormons' neighbors, began in temple ceremonies in Kirtland, Ohio. It

In 1831, Smith moved the church to Kirtland, Ohio, where the Kirtland Temple was built.

is called "sealing"—spiritual marriage. Sealing means that a "marriage covenant between a man and his wife is made for time and all eternity," not like most marriage covenants that are regarded "until death shall them part."[2] This belief also means that families can be "sealed" to one another and will be together after death.

Another practice perceived as irreverent by many Christians is baptism for the dead. A baptismal font is constructed in temples for this purpose. For the ordinance, a person acting by proxy is ceremonially baptized in the name of a deceased person. (Mormons believe that the deceased person has the opportunity to accept or reject the baptism performed on his or her behalf. They believe that baptism is a ceremony that must be performed on earth.)

This practice led to the genealogical work that is associated with Mormons today. Members search out the names of their dead ancestors to perform baptisms in their name and to do temple work for them, including marriages and other ordinances they believe necessary for their dead ancestors to return to God. Today, the church has the largest collection of genealogical records in the world.

Not everyone can enter Mormon temples. Only members in good standing, as defined by the doctrine, can enter temples and perform ordinances in them. After completing certain ceremonies in the temple, members wear "garments," a type of under-clothing. Worn under regular clothing, the garment serves as a guide for modesty of dress and has other sacred significance. The garment covers the torso and the upper portion of the thighs. It has small sleeves. Mormons wear garments at all times except during bathing and swimming.

Observance of the Word of Wisdom is another practice the Mormons' neighbors found unusual. It is still associated with church practice today. Perhaps the best known of Smith's revelations, it suggests abstinence from alcohol, tobacco, and hot drinks—which Mormons interpret as tea and coffee—and restricts the use of wine for communion only. It also recommends that meat be eaten only in winter—later interpreted to mean meat should be eaten in limited amounts.

The guideline at first was taken as advice, not commandment. The code received lax interpretation until the 1880s, when it "became a prerequisite for appointment to leadership positions, service as missionaries, and entrance into the temples," according to Mormon historians Leonard J. Arrington and Davis Bitton.[3]

Eventually, water was substituted for wine in the sacrament (communion), and abstention from tobacco, coffee, tea, and liquor was necessary for being considered a member in good standing.

Mormons were not the only ones suggesting that alcoholic beverages and meat in diets be restricted. Smith said he received the revelation in 1833, a time when the activities of temperance societies, which worked to outlaw alcoholic beverages, were rising. Five thousand temperance associations were active in the United States by 1834. It was also a time when concern for health through dietary measures was becoming popular.

But the doctrine that brought the Mormons their biggest problems in the early years of the church and would continue to haunt them later was polygamy. The church said that some men had the right to have more than one wife at a time. (Women, however, could not have multiple husbands.)

Leaders of the church said that Smith had told them in the 1830s that plural marriage was a "correct principle."[4] The doctrine was taught secretly and practiced only by church leaders, including Smith, at the beginning.

Smith secretly recorded the doctrine on July 12, 1843. However, the church officially denied that it had a policy of plural marriage—even though it was practiced—until 1852, when polygamy was formally acknowledged by leaders headquartered in Salt Lake City, Utah.

Polygamy, sealing, baptism for the dead, and multiple gods, all helped fuel distrust of the Mormons in the early years of the church. As Mormon historians have pointed out, "A group that succeeds in turning friends and the far more numerous 'neutrals' into enemies, as the Mormons did in one place after another, must have exhibited some repellent characteristics, at the very least."[5]

GENTILES VERSUS SAINTS

In the summer of 1831, Joseph Smith said it had been revealed to him that the Mormons should establish a community in western Missouri.

An advance company, mostly converts from Colesville, New York, headed west. They floated on flatboats up the Missouri River to the Big Blue District, twelve miles west of Independence, Missouri.

Smith followed the advance party of Mormons west in June 1831. In nearby Independence, Smith selected the site for a temple and ground was broken for the holy city of Zion, the New Jerusalem.

Ultimatum Delivered

Meanwhile, hostility toward the Mormons was brewing in Missouri. Their claim that God had given them the land and that it would someday be free of Gentiles—a word Mormons used for nonmembers—angered and frightened the Missourians. Resentment grew as more and more Mormons, whom the settlers considered religious zealots, moved into the area.

The Mormons' first indication of trouble in Missouri came in the spring of 1832. Several homes were stoned, and families were harassed at night by raiders on horseback. The harassment became more aggressive; gunshots were fired into cabins, and a haystack owned by the church was burned.

Change came abruptly in July, when W. W. Phelps, editor of the *Evening and Morning Star*, wrote an article titled "Free People of Color." A convert to the church, Phelps was a poet and journalist from New York. The *Star* had been established by Smith to publish his revelations and letters and to help spread the word of his church in Missouri.

Phelps's article enraged the Missourians. They believed he was inviting freed slaves to come to their state and was instructing them on how to do it. They did not like the fact that Mormons opposed slavery. Missourians were already uncomfortable with the Mormons' sympathetic attitudes toward the American Indians. This talk of abolition (ending slavery) was the last straw.

A group of Missourians met and wrote a manifesto that declared their intentions to "rid our society, 'peaceably if we can, forcibly if we must,' . . . [of these] deluded fanatics."[1]

Five hundred settlers held a meeting on July 20, 1833, and demanded the expulsion of the Mormons. The settlers waited outside the courthouse while a committee of twelve men served Mormon leaders with the notice. The Mormons tried to explain to the delegation that church authorities in Kirtland had to be notified before a decision could be made. They asked for three months to reply.

When the waiting settlers heard the Mormons' response, they turned into an angry mob. They immediately rode off for the Mormon community west of town and headed straight for Phelps's house, where the printing press was located. They forced Phelps and his family into the street, smashed furniture, tore the press apart, threw its pieces out the door, and destroyed the two-story brick building. They carried off copies of the Book of Commandments, a compilation of Smith's revelations, and destroyed them.

Three days later, the message was reiterated with a public warning to all Jackson County Mormons. A group of Missourians rode into Independence, waving whips and rifles, promising to burn crops and flog Mormons on sight until their demands were met.

To avoid more violence, Mormon leaders agreed to evacuate half the Mormon families by January 1, 1834, and promised that all Mormons would be out of Jackson County by April 1.

Blood and Death

On September 28, 1833, Mormon leaders petitioned Missouri Governor Daniel Dunklin to dispatch troops to maintain order while the matter was handled in the courts. They then filed lawsuits for property damage.

Dunklin's reply on October 19 was sympathetic but denied their request for military protection. He suggested that they rely on the courts to settle their grievances. Dunklin's decision had been influenced by Lieutenant Governor Lilburn W. Boggs, an outspoken critic of the Mormons.

When the Missourians found out that the Mormons planned to fight the Jackson County evacuation notice in court, the mobs again rose up. An eight-day reign of terror—beatings, destruction, and death—began on the night of October 31, 1833.

The Mormon community in the Big Blue District was attacked by fifty settlers. Men were clubbed, stoned, and beaten with whips and guns. Women and children ran screaming into the woods. Many cabins were damaged; more than thirteen were unroofed.

In a second assault on the Big Blue District, a group of raiders from west of the settlement teamed with a group from Independence. When darkness fell, they surrounded the Mormon settlement and moved in. Some of the raiders had stripped to the waist and painted themselves to look like Indians.

Ropes were looped over the eaves of a building and tied to saddle pummels. As the horses moved forward, the cabin was unroofed with a loud crack.

On November 3, on the outskirts of Independence, thirty Mormons armed with guns surprised raiders en route to the Big Blue District, and two Missourians were killed.

Lieutenant Governor Boggs persuaded Governor Dunklin to call out the militia to restore order. The governor put in charge Colonel Thomas Pitcher, who had signed the settlers' manifesto against the Mormons.

The Mormons again gathered in force outside Independence. There, they encountered Boggs with the colonel and his militia. The colonel insisted that the Mormons surrender and demanded that several men give themselves up to be tried for the murder of the two raiders. Boggs personally urged the Mormons to disarm and promised that the colonel and his militia would also disarm the mob. The church leaders agreed.

Evacuation

The settlers, however, were never disarmed, and the news that the Mormons were without weapons spread like wildfire. Raiders attacked every Mormon community, destroying homes, beating and whipping men, driving women and children out, and threatening the Mormons with death if they did not leave Jackson County.

A fierce, biting November wind accompanied the twelve hundred Mormons who had been driven from their homes as they made their way to the banks of the Missouri River.

By November 7, 1833, nearly one thousand Mormons were still waiting for a turn on the ferry that was shuttling them across the river to Clay County. The boat was frequently forced to halt because storms whipped the water, making safe passage impossible.

Joseph Smith organized his Mormon followers in military divisions to defend themselves against the attacks of local settlers who disapproved of their religious beliefs.

Hungry, cold, and tired, the Mormons camped on the riverbank and looked for a sign that their God had not forsaken them. Before dawn on November 18, 1833, they looked up to see the night sky light up. Thousands of meteors with long tails of light shot through the darkness for several hours. The Mormons were witnessing the Leonid meteor shower, which peaks around November 17 each year. The Mormons took the meteor display as a sign that all would be well, that one day they would be able to resettle in Jackson County and reclaim their divine heritage.

Outside Reaction

The violence against the Mormons brought them their first sympathetic public reaction. The Missouri press deplored the mob behavior, and newspapers across the nation carried stories about the incidents and wrote editorials about the unjust treatment of the Mormons.

Few other minority religions had ever attracted the type of persecution Mormons experienced from state to state. The cause of the strong reactions from their neighbors is complex.

The social system implemented by the church was part of it. The communistic approach to social organization, or the United Order, was a system Smith also called the Law of Consecration and Stewardship. Members deeded all their property to the church and received "inheritances," or land, that they managed. Surplus was distributed by the bishop—leader of an area—to the poor and those without property.

This social system also had economic consequences. The concept of common property challenged the young nation's enthusiasm for free enterprise and was seen by many as un-American. Another economic factor was that Mormons traded mostly with other Mormons. They traded with local merchants only when there was no other way for them to get the supplies they needed. But even that little outside trade subsided as Mormons became more self-sufficient.

Potential political consequences were also troubling for non-Mormons. Since the Mormons were easterners who did not own slaves, they were a voting bloc that threatened the Missourians' way of life. Also, fear that elected officials would be Mormons or people sympathetic to Mormons worried the settlers.

Finally, the Missourians, whose frontier state bordered Indian Territory, did not share the Mormons' love for the American Indians. Many non-Mormons interpreted Mormon beliefs as nothing more than superstitions, and many found their beliefs repellent. The Mormons, unaffected by outside reaction, believed that Jackson County, Missouri, was their divine heritage, their Zion. They would attempt to regain the property they had been forced to leave.

The displaced Mormons remained in Clay County, Missouri, north of the Missouri River. At first, the Mormons were welcomed and given temporary shelter. Fearing the same conflicts would eventually arise once again, the Missouri state legislature created two new northern counties and designated one for the

Mormons. On the move again, the Mormons made Caldwell County, Missouri, their new home in 1836.

Far West

When Joseph Smith and Sidney Rigdon reached Far West in Caldwell County, Missouri, in January 1838, they found a village of nearly one hundred fifty log cabins, which included four dry-goods stores, six blacksmith shops, nine family groceries, and two hotels.

But Smith's troubles were not left at the county line. A group of dissenters (people who reject the doctrines of a church) had rebelled against Smith and were living in Caldwell County. They had openly accused Smith of being a false prophet, thief, and adulterer.

The Caldwell County faithful wanted the dissenters out of the settlement. Smith and church leaders in Far West decided that the dissenters had to leave, but they did not know how to get rid of them. Finally, Rigdon drafted a document notifying the dissenters that they had three days to pack up and leave. It was signed by eighty-three of the most influential Mormons of Caldwell County.

Danites

In June 1838, a secret society of Mormon men was formed to ferret out dissenters and to protect against possible aggression from Missouri settlers. Since the slavery issue would not go away—the majority of Mormons opposed it—many people within the church believed they needed to be prepared to defend themselves. The group called itself the Sons of Dan, or Danites. Organized in military fashion, its members devised secret signs and passwords to be used in times of danger, and they swore oaths of secrecy.

Smith denied knowledge of the Danites until the group's existence was disclosed in a court proceeding in 1838. But from its conception, the organization played a dominant role in the early years of the church.

An example of the group's influence in the community came in July 1838 when Smith said he had a revelation that surplus property—anything more than a family needed for survival—would belong to the church communally. Sampson Avard, organizer of the Danites, threatened Mormons who hesitated. He made clear his interpretation of the Danites' role in the community: They were to be the enforcers of the Lord's counsel.

Elections

About thirty Mormons left Caldwell County on August 6, 1838, election day in Missouri, to vote for the first time in five years. William P. Peniston, candidate for the state legislature, was an outspoken anti-Mormon. Fearing the Mormon vote might defeat him, he had organized a mob to prevent the Mormons from voting.

When the Mormons arrived at the polls, three hundred Missourians were listening to Peniston, who was on a tirade about the Mormons, calling them horse thieves, liars, and counterfeiters. He warned the settlers, "If you suffer the Mormons to vote in this election, it will mean the end of your suffrage [right to vote]."[2]

When the first Mormon walked toward the polls to vote, a settler blocked his path, told him they did not allow Mormons or African Americans to vote, and knocked him down. Another Mormon came to the aid of the first, and a fight broke out. The remaining Mormons grabbed oak boards to arm themselves.

When the Danite signal of distress was flashed, all the Mormons wielded their clubs and attacked the settlers. Nine Missourians lay stretched on the ground while others, bruised and bleeding, crawled away.

No one was killed, but exaggerated reports of the incident spread quickly. News came to Far West that the justice of the peace in the town of Gallatin was organizing an army to expel the residents of the Mormon town of Adam-ondi-Ahman in Daviess County.

Smith immediately organized troops in Far West and set out for Adam-ondi-Ahman. When he reached the settlement, he learned that the reports he had heard about the incident at the polls had been misleading, but he decided to confront the justice of the peace anyway.

Upon reaching the justice's home, the Mormons demanded that he sign a peace agreement with them. He refused. They threatened him with violence. He agreed and penned a note promising to uphold the United States and state constitutions. Satisfied, the Mormons rode off.

The Mormons' visit to the justice's home infuriated the Missourians. A warrant was issued against Smith and another Mormon leader for threatening the justice's life. The two men were brought in and released after posting bail.

This was not good enough for the Missourians. Settlers from eleven counties and four hundred militiamen called out by Lilburn W. Boggs, now governor of Missouri, planned to take Smith by force.

The Mormons surprised the Missourians by making the first move. They sent a raiding party to intercept a shipment of ammunition and guns headed for the settlers in Daviess County.

Boggs declared a state of insurrection (an uprising against established authority). He ordered militia commanders to march on the Mormons and stop the uprising.

The Missourians attacked Mormon settlements. DeWitt, a river port fifty miles south of the town of Far West, was put under siege. The next day, October 3, 1838, Adam-ondi-Ahman was raided. Flogged Mormons were left tied to trees.

In retaliation, the Mormons simultaneously struck the towns of Gallatin, Millport, and Grindstone Fork. The Missourians were caught off guard. The Mormons raided and took what they could from the settlers. When successful raids brought wagon loads of stolen goods back to Mormon settlements, some Mormons found the theft so outrageous that they packed up their families and left.

To release three Mormons who had been taken captive by the state militia and to thwart a threatened attack on Far West, Smith planned a surprise attack on state militia forces camped at Crooked River.

An hour before dawn, sixty Mormons positioned themselves along the river embankment. A militia guard spotted a silhouette of one of them against the night sky, fired, and killed him. The Mormons charged.

The surprised militia fell under the heated attack. When it was over, three Mormons and one militiaman lay dead. But the exaggerated report that reached Governor Boggs told of a massacre by the Mormons.

Boggs also received sworn statements from two former Mormon leaders, Thomas B. Marsh and Orson Hyde, who were among those who had left because of the Mormons' raiding and looting. Marsh and Hyde exposed the Danites and disclosed their plans to attack.

Boggs, warned by one of his generals that civil war was inevitable, on October 27, 1838, issued an extermination order—an order to kill—in a letter to General John B. Clark:

> Your orders are to hasten your operations and endeavor to reach Richmond, in Ray County, with all possible speed. The Mormons must be treated as enemies and must be exterminated or driven from the state, if necessary for the public good. Their outrages are beyond all description.[3]

Smith Surrenders

On the afternoon of October 30, 1838, a militia of about eight hundred men camped outside Far West. A messenger from the camp brought Smith a copy of Bogg's extermination order and a warning that six thousand more men were on their way.

Smith could see that his options were limited. The Mormons were outnumbered five-to-one and more militiamen were coming. The next morning, he arranged a meeting between his representatives and the commander of the militia. One of the terms imposed by the militia for surrender was that Smith and four other Mormon leaders be taken immediately as hostages.

When Smith and the others failed to surrender, the militia moved forward, and the Mormons braced for battle. When the militia was six hundred yards from the low wall the Mormons had erected to defend themselves, Joseph Smith and four other leaders— Sidney Rigdon, Parley Pratt, Lyman Wight, and George W. Robinson—surrendered to prevent the inevitable battle and loss of Mormon lives. At the sight of their white flag, cheers rose from the ranks of the militia.

The prisoners spent the night on the hard ground in the rain, taunted by their guards. Around midnight, one of the generals, Samuel Lucas, told Wight that they would all be shot in the morning in Far West's public square.

The Escape

Word spread quickly among Mormons in Far West that their leaders had surrendered. Twenty-seven of the men who had fought at Crooked River fled into Illinois that night, seeking protection.

Alexander Doniphan, a militia general and lawyer who had helped the Mormons five years earlier in Jackson County, declared he would not be part of the execution and threatened to remove his brigade.

His action caused the other generals to rethink their position, and instead of being executed, Smith and the other prisoners were transferred to Independence to stand trial on charges of "several crimes of high treason against the state, murder, arson, burglary, robbery and larceny."[4]

Chained to each other, the church leaders and about forty other Mormons were tried in Missouri's Fifth Judicial District in Richmond. The witnesses against them included other Mormons who testified to the existence of the Danites.

The judge was not able to identify any laws prohibiting membership in such an organization, so most of the defendants were granted bail or released. Four were retained at Richmond Jail. Joseph and Hyrum Smith, Rigdon, and three other Mormon leaders were sent to Liberty Jail in Clay County to await trial.

During Smith's five-month stay in jail, which began on November 30, 1838, he and the other Mormon leaders twice attempted to escape but failed. On April 12, 1839, Smith, his brother Hyrum, and the

Joseph Smith, his brother Hyrum, Rigdon, and three other Mormon leaders were sent to Liberty Jail to await trial on charges of high treason, murder, arson, and burglary.

three other church leaders faced a grand jury in Gallatin, which indicted them for "murder, treason, burglary, arson, larceny, theft and stealing."[5] (Due to failing health, Rigdon had been granted bail earlier and had joined church members in Quincy, Illinois.)

Three days later, the court unexpectedly ordered the men to be taken to Boone County for sentencing. It was evident that the move was a deliberate attempt to allow the prisoners a chance to make a break. Apparently, government officials realized that letting them escape would be a solution. It was obvious that Smith and the others would leave the state and unlikely that they would ever return with a grand jury indictment hanging over their heads.

The five Mormon leaders did escape during the transfer and rode into Quincy, Illinois, on April 22, 1839. They had become fugitives from the state of Missouri.

With the Missouri governor's extermination order hanging over their heads, the Mormons crossed the Mississippi River by ferry to Quincy, Illinois. The residents were hospitable and sympathetic for the most part. However, some were not so enthusiastic about the outsiders. In *Recollections of a Little Girl in the Forties*, Mary Jane Selby, an Illinois resident, compared the Mormons to a disease. "There were several not very desirable events that occurred in Quincy," she wrote. "One was the advent of a large number of refugee Mormons, driven out of Missouri. Another unwelcome visitor that I remember was the invasion of cholera."[1]

THE CITY OF JOSEPH

The refugees numbered between twelve thousand and fifteen thousand. There was no way that the small town of Quincy could absorb them all. Some Mormon leaders suggested splitting up, but Brigham Young, president of the Quorum of the Twelve Apostles, one of the governing bodies of the church, argued against it. When Joseph Smith arrived on April 22, 1839, he made his will known: The Mormons would settle together, and a new Zion would be formed outside Quincy.

Nauvoo

Smith immediately set out to purchase land for the New Jerusalem. He bought property in Illinois and more land across the Mississippi River in Iowa.

About ten miles north of Quincy, the winding Mississippi had cut an arc of land with three miles of river frontage. The riverbank rose enough to allow a view of the great, glimmering semicircle shaped by the river. This area, including a small community called Commerce, was to be the Mormons' new Zion. Smith renamed the town Nauvoo and told his followers that the name meant "a beautiful plantation" in Hebrew.[2]

The growth of the city far surpassed anything the Mormons had ever experienced. After one year, Nauvoo had two hundred fifty houses and a corner-stone for a temple that was to be built on the summit of a hill overlooking the river. Charters were drawn up to incorporate the new city.

Interested in winning the Mormon vote, politicians of both the Whig and Democratic parties were easy game for Dr. John Cook Bennett, an 1840 convert who lobbied for a favorable vote on the proposed charters. Passing both houses of the legislature on a voice vote, the charters for Nauvoo represented Smith's first political victory.

Grateful, Smith created the position of assistant president of the church for Bennett and named him

After fleeing Missouri, the Mormons moved to Illinois, where they set up their church and built the Nauvoo Temple (the building at top with the spire).

mayor of Nauvoo. Smith also appointed Bennett chancellor of the University of Nauvoo and brigadier general of the Nauvoo Legion, second in command to Smith himself.

The high visibility of the Legion, which paraded regularly, created a military atmosphere that permeated the city. It was the duty of every man between the ages of eighteen and forty-five to join. By January 1842, the militia had more than two thousand members. Total church membership was more than thirty thousand. Bennett was quartermaster general of the Illinois state militia, and he used that position to obtain three cannons and about two hundred fifty small arms for the Nauvoo Legion.

The boys of the city organized their own military group and between four hundred and six hundred of them paraded and drilled with an enthusiasm that equaled that of their fathers.

Dissent Without and Within

The church's doctrines, together with old political problems—Mormons represented a powerful voting bloc—brought renewed opposition. Thomas Sharp, the editor of the *Warsaw Signal*, an Illinois paper, attacked the Mormons for their economic exclusiveness, bloc voting, and unorthodox beliefs.

Opposition to doctrine was not limited to outsiders. Within the church, a group of dissenters emerged. Headed by William Law, a member of the church's leadership, it held traditional concepts of family and marriage and opposed polygamy.

Law, Dr. Robert D. Foster, and brothers Francis and Chauncey Higbee broke away from Smith, organized a new church, and named Law their prophet. They ordered a printing press and circulated a prospectus among the citizens of Nauvoo that described their goals and their plans to print a weekly newspaper. The prospectus explained that they advocated the repeal of the Nauvoo city charter, and they planned to expose "the many *gross abuses exercised under the pretended authorities of the Nauvoo City Charter*."[3]

The dissenters also took legal action against Smith. Law testified before a grand jury in Carthage, which resulted in an indictment against Smith on charges of adultery.

The first issue of the *Nauvoo Expositor* was circulated on June 7, 1844. It contained a reprint of the prospectus, an exposé of plural marriage, charges of immorality against Smith for practicing polygamy, and criticism of his pretensions to national office (Smith had declared himself a candidate for president of the United States in the 1844 campaign).

Smith called a special session of the city council and obtained an ordinance prohibiting libel (words or pictures that expose a person to public disgrace or ridicule, or create an ill opinion of him or her) under penalty of a $5,000 fine and six months in jail. Smith then told council members to gather testimony about the reputations of the newspaper publishers, and he pushed through a motion stating that, under the new libel law, the *Nauvoo Expositor* was a public nuisance. The mayor was ordered by the city council to remove the printing press and destroy the newspapers.

Smith joined the posse, made up of members of the Nauvoo Legion, and marched to the newspaper office. Foster and Chauncey Higbee locked the door, met them out front, and refused to surrender the key. Smith gave a signal, and Orrin Porter Rockwell—Smith's bodyguard, a Danite, and a man Smith once referred to as the "Destroying Angel"—kicked the door off its hinges.[4] Seven men struggled to pull the press into the street. The heap of rubble was soaked in coal oil and set on fire.

It had been an eventful day, beginning with the special council meeting and ending with the destruction of the opposition press. However, Smith's decision to destroy the rival newspaper was the beginning of the end for the first prophet of the Church of Jesus Christ of Latter-day Saints.

Lamb to the Slaughter

Throughout the region, destruction of the newspaper became a freedom of the press issue, and Smith found himself cast in the role of oppressor.

Believing their lives to be in danger, Foster and Law, the publishers of the destroyed newspaper, fled to Carthage, Illinois. There, they initiated legal action against Smith and the Nauvoo City Council, charging them with rioting.

A constable who was sent to arrest Joseph and Hyrum Smith was met with pleas from the Mormons for the brothers not to be tried in Carthage. Fearing that if they were taken to Carthage they would not return alive, Joseph Smith successfully secured a writ of habeas corpus (a document requiring that a detained person be brought before a court to decide the legality of the detention). The Smiths were tried and acquitted in Nauvoo by a non-Mormon judge who was sympathetic to their fears.

When the constable returned to Carthage empty-handed, the settlers were enraged. Vigilante groups from Illinois, Iowa, and Missouri began organizing, determined to correct what they saw as Smith's defiance of the law.

When word reached Smith of the settlers' plans, he mobilized the Nauvoo Legion and declared martial law in Nauvoo. News of his reaction filtered back to the settlers, and they sent demands to Illinois Governor Thomas Ford to use the state militia to bring Smith to justice.

Ford traveled to Carthage, reviewed the evidence, and declared Smith's destruction of the newspaper illegal. He suggested that the Smiths surrender on the original charge of rioting. Joseph Smith agreed to face the charge, even though he considered it double jeopardy (being tried twice for the same crime), but only if he were allowed an armed escort of his own men.

In the meantime, to Ford's dismay, a settlers' militia had assembled in Carthage and was prepared to march on the orders of the local constable. Fearing civil war would erupt if the Nauvoo Legion accompanied Smith to Carthage, Ford denied Smith's request and warned him that if he refused to surrender, Nauvoo might be destroyed and many Mormons killed. "You know the excitement of the public mind. Do not tempt it too far," Ford told Smith.[5]

Smith Surrenders

On June 24, 1844, Joseph and Hyrum Smith and several other Mormon leaders who were also wanted by the law rode toward Carthage, accompanied by the Nauvoo Legion. At the edge of the city, they were met by a company of Mormons from Ramus, a town east of Nauvoo, who had come to join the Nauvoo Legion. The men from Ramus had marched all night to escort their prophet.

As they made their way toward Carthage, Smith told his companions, "I am going like a lamb to the slaughter. . . . I SHALL DIE INNOCENT, AND IT SHALL YET BE SAID OF ME—HE WAS MURDERED IN COLD BLOOD."[6]

A militia from McDonough County met them along the route to escort them on the final leg of their journey. Upon arrival in Carthage, about midnight, they were greeted with taunts and death threats from a militia group from Warsaw and the Carthage militia, whose members were called Greys.

Once jailed, Joseph and Hyrum Smith were informed that in addition to the charge of rioting, they faced charges of treason because Smith had declared martial law in Nauvoo.

At a preliminary hearing on the charge of rioting, all cases were deferred, and everyone but Joseph and Hyrum Smith was released on bail. The brothers were put back in jail on charges of treason and levying war against the state.

Life in Carthage Jail

Even though he disliked the Mormons and believed Smith to be a fake, Illinois Governor Ford was determined to have a legal trial.

Ford permitted the brothers to stay in an unbarred apartment on the second floor of the Carthage jail. He also allowed Smith's friends to visit him, which enabled messages to be smuggled.

Joseph and Hyrum Smith were taken before a Carthage judge late on the afternoon of June 26. They were escorted outside and through a group of Carthage Greys, who had made no secret of their dislike of the Mormons. Smith was convinced they would be killed any second as they walked down the row of agitated, angry militiamen.

An hour of legal maneuvering resulted in a request by the defendants to continue the case in the morning. The judge granted the motion. As the brothers were returning to the jail, all but two of their visitors— Willard Richards and John Taylor, both members of the Quorum of the Twelve Apostles—were turned

Joseph Smith and his brother Hyrum were held in the Carthage jail while awaiting trial.

away at bayonet point and not allowed to accompany them back to the jail.

The next morning, June 27, 1844, Ford rode to Nauvoo to address the Mormons, leaving a detachment of the Carthage Greys to guard the jail.

Final Hours

Most of the Greys were camped about a quarter of a mile from the jail; eight of them were stationed at the site. About five o'clock in the afternoon, Joseph and Hyrum Smith, along with their two companions, Richards and Taylor, finished dinner and "sent for a bottle of wine, some pipes, and two small papers of

tobacco with which to pass the time."⁷ (The Word of
Wisdom, which prohibited use of tobacco and alcohol,
was regarded as advice, not commandment, at this
time.)

After the delivery, as the guard headed back down
the stairs, the Mormon leaders heard someone call to
him. That was followed by shouts to surrender and a
quick succession of gunshots. Richards ran to the window and saw the courtyard filled with armed men.
The mob of about one hundred fifty men consisted
mostly of the Warsaw militia. They had escorted the
governor out of town, then waited until he was out of
sight before returning to join the Carthage Greys.

The Greys' guns were loaded with blanks, so that
they could fire upon the invading Warsaw militia to
create the appearance of attempting to protect the
Smiths. Some members of the Warsaw militia opened
fire on the Smiths' cell from the courtyard below while
others ran into the building and up the stairs.

Two guns had been smuggled into the prison by
Smith's visitors the day before. When the gunfire
began, Joseph Smith grabbed a six-shooter and
Hyrum a single-barrel pistol. Richards and Taylor were
armed only with their canes.

With faces blackened in disguise, members of the
Warsaw militia stormed up the stairs. The prisoners
and the militia exchanged gunfire through the door. A
bullet hit Hyrum in the nose. As he stumbled, he was
struck in the back by bullets coming through the
window. "I am a dead man!" he shouted before he died.⁸

Hyrum Smith, Joseph Smith's brother, was killed in the raid by the local settlers against the jailed Mormon leaders.

Reaching around the doorpost, Joseph Smith fired six times. Two or three of the gun's chambers misfired, but the others found their targets, and three of the assailants were wounded. Wildly swinging their canes, Taylor and Richards hit the gun hands of the attackers as they forced their way into the room.

Taylor, realizing the situation was hopeless, headed for the window. A bullet hit his left thigh, and he fell across the sill. A shot from outside hit the watch in his vest pocket and knocked him back into the room. He was hit twice more before he managed to roll under a bed, where he was hit by a fifth bullet.

Joseph Smith ran to the window. Two shots, fired from the doorway, hit him in the back. A third, fired from the courtyard below, entered his chest. As he clung to the windowsill, he cried, "Oh Lord, my

God!"[9] He then dropped twenty-five feet to the ground below.

Richards stood alone inside the bloodstained jail cell, bleeding from his only injury—a bullet had grazed his neck and left earlobe. He moved to the window and watched the crowd gathering around his dying prophet. Taylor, still lying under the bed, called out to Richards, "Take me."[10]

Richards dragged the severely wounded man to an adjacent room. They heard the sounds of men running back up the stairs, and listened silently as the men came upon Hyrum's body in the next room. Then, from outside the prison, came shouts of, "The Mormons are coming! The Mormons are coming!"[11] The men quickly fled down the stairs.

John Taylor was seriously wounded in the attack against Mormon leaders at the Carthage jail, but he survived.

While Richards attempted to make his wounded friend comfortable, he noticed Taylor's shattered watch. The bullet had stopped the watch and recorded the hour that would become part of Mormon history— five o'clock, sixteen minutes, and twenty-six seconds.

Before the men in the courtyard scattered, a barefoot man made his way through the mob to the Mormon prophet. He dragged Smith to a curb a few feet from the jail and propped him up.

When Smith stirred and opened his eyes, four men were ordered by Warsaw militia colonel Levi Williams, a local minister, to fire at him. The muskets, eight feet from their target, fired simultaneously. A slight tremor shook Smith's body, then he fell forward on his face, dead.

The mob dispersed, and the prophet's body lay alone. Richards finally left the prison room, carried Smith's body back into the jail, and laid the brothers' bodies next to each other. He sent for help for the wounded Taylor and found a messenger to take the news of the murders to Nauvoo.

Though the first prophet of the Latter-day Saints was dead, the church did not die, as many thought it would. Instead, it grew to a membership of more than 10 million by the end of the nineteenth century.

6

FINAL EXODUS

Brigham Young, who organized the evacuation of the Mormons from Missouri while Joseph Smith was in jail, would face the awesome task of leading the Mormons on an even more dramatic exodus—a journey of more than thirteen hundred miles from Nauvoo, across the western plains, to the Rocky Mountains.

Young was recognized as a natural leader with an amazing ability to organize and govern. In addition to eventually becoming president of the Church of Jesus Christ of Latter-day Saints, he would become the first governor of Utah. The members of the church, under his direction, would play a significant role in the settlement of the West—not only present-day Utah, but California, Idaho, Arizona, and Nevada, as well.

The ninth child of John and Nabby Howe Young, Brigham Young was born on June 1, 1801, in the town of Whitingham, Vermont. When he was a boy, his very poor family moved from New England to New York.

Brigham's mother died when he was fourteen, leaving him with his strict father, of whom Young said, "It used to be a word and blow with him, but the blows came first."[1] Instead of continuing his schooling, Brigham became an apprentice and learned the skills of a carpenter, painter, and glazier (a person who cuts glass and sets it in windows).

Brigham Young was attracted to the church after he read the Book of Mormon. He met Smith in November 1832. Chopping wood in the forest behind his house, Smith paused while his friends introduced him to Young, a new convert. Smith immediately recognized Young's leadership potential.

Young's intelligence and charisma quickly moved him into church leadership positions. Brigham Young, whom Smith called "The Lion of the Lord," was president of the Twelve Apostles when Smith was killed.[2]

Brigham Young joined the church in 1832.

The Prophet Is Buried

More than ten thousand men and women—many weeping, many crying out for revenge—lined the streets of Nauvoo early on the morning of June 28, 1844, as the bodies of their prophet, Joseph Smith, and his brother Hyrum were brought home.

After a viewing at Smith's home, the mourners left and the coffins were removed from the outer pine boxes that held them. Fearing desecration of the graves by anti-Mormons, leaders of the church put sand in the original coffins, took them to the cemetery, and buried them.

As midnight approached, the brothers' bodies, which had been hidden in a locked bedroom, were carried to the Nauvoo House, a hotel still under construction. There, they were buried in the basement.

The devastating death of their prophet, coupled with the fact that no orderly means of succession for leadership had been clearly established, created a divisive climate among the Mormons.

The Mantle of Joseph Smith

Upon news of Smith's murder, most of the Twelve Apostles were immediately called home. Smith had sent them on missions to bring converts into the church and to push for his candidacy for president of the United States.

Sidney Rigdon, who had been campaigning in Pittsburgh, was the only member of the First Presidency (the president of the church and his two counselors) still alive. Returning to Nauvoo, he announced in a Sunday service that he had received a vision telling him that no man could take Smith's place, but that he, Rigdon, should be recognized as "guardian," or interim president, of the church.[3] Brigham Young argued that he, as president of the Apostles, should become prophet.

The Smith family, however, had no patience with the logic of either Rigdon or Young. Quoting statements Smith had made about his son assuming leadership of the church, they said that eleven-year-old Joseph Smith III should succeed the slain prophet, with the boy's uncle, William Smith, serving in the position until Joseph came of age.

Both Rigdon and Young delivered rousing speeches at a general meeting of the Nauvoo congregation, each hoping to convince members that he should take the reins of the church. During Young's impassioned speech, those present said Young's "voice was the voice of Br[other] Joseph and his face appeared as Joseph's face."[4]

Young's plea was followed by others who supported the argument that the new leader should come from the Twelve Apostles. After the stirring presentations, the membership, in an overwhelming vote, endorsed Young as their new president and prophet.

Wolf Hunt

The shock of the murders of Joseph and Hyrum Smith created a period of lowered tensions between the

Mormons and their neighbors. But the calm lasted only a short time. Old conflicts soon resurfaced. The Mormons' neighbors again saw them as radical and incompatible with Christian standards.

By the winter of 1844–1845, non-Mormons were accusing the Mormons of stealing. The Mormons denied the charges and countered with the claim that non-Mormons had planted stolen goods in Nauvoo to frame them.

In response to the alleged thefts, the settlers planned raids against Mormons that they called "wolf hunts."[5] Word passed throughout Nauvoo that the settlers were going to burn the Mormons out.

Elected officials were of no help. Neither the Whig party nor the Democratic party was willing to risk losing votes by showing too much sympathy toward the Mormons.

As the tension grew, Young prepared the Mormons for battle. An arsenal was opened and the Nauvoo Legion started regular drills. News of Young's preparations filtered out, and the settlers contacted militia captains in Iowa, Missouri, and neighboring counties in Illinois, inviting them to join the wolf hunts.

To the raiders' surprise, however, they were forced to disband when Governor Ford sent a volunteer state militia of five hundred men to ward off the arrival of the neighboring militia groups. Ford wanted to avoid armed conflict between the settlers and the Mormons.

There was little rest, however. The next month, the

anti-Mormon paper, *Warsaw Signal*, and the Mormons' *Nauvoo Neighbor* flung accusations back and forth.

But the most damaging blow struck against the Mormons was more than an accusation. In an attempt to cripple the Mormons legally and thereby gain control over the city of Nauvoo, the Illinois state legislature revoked the city's charter, which had granted the Mormons so much power, including the right to raise a militia.

Surrounded by problems, it was becoming clear to Young that conditions were quickly getting worse for the Mormons, and there was no reason to believe they would ever get any better. If the future did not look bleak enough, more bad news came their way. After a twelve-day trial that began on May 19, 1845, the defendants on trial for the murders of Joseph and Hyrum Smith were found not guilty.

By the fall, several months after the verdict, mob violence had flared up again. Bands of raiders set fire to Mormons' houses, buildings, barns, and grain. The Danites responded with both defensive and aggressive actions, and the report that reached the governor's desk was that the Mormons had "sallied forth and ravaged the country" in retaliation.[6]

In the meantime, Young and one of his governing councils dispatched a group of men to investigate the west side of the Rocky Mountains, known as the Great Basin or the Great Salt Lake valley, to determine whether it could become their new home.

Before Smith died, he had read reports about several areas in the West—Oregon, Texas, and California—for possible settlement. Young reviewed the information that Smith had accumulated and studied explorer John C. Frémont's report on an 1843–1844 expedition into Utah, southern Oregon, and California, and his exploration into present-day Colorado and Wyoming.

On September 9, 1845, the same night the decision was made to investigate the West, a non-Mormon community called Green Plains was attacked. Though Young claimed that the attack had been made by non-Mormons as an excuse to declare war on the Mormons, the settlers vowed vengeance.

The night skies were lit by the flames of burning Mormon homes—forty-four had been destroyed by September 15. Anti-Mormon sentiment was so strong that when the sheriff attempted to raise a posse to go after the raiders, not one volunteer came forward. He then approached Young for help, and two thousand men from the Nauvoo Legion marched across the county. As word of the coming Legion reached them, many settlers fled Illinois for Missouri and Iowa.

Flames dotted the countryside. Non-Mormon as well as Mormon property was destroyed. Fearing civil war, Governor Ford sent four hundred troops to Hancock County with a committee authorized to negotiate with Young. On October 1, 1845, Young made his decision public—the Mormons were leaving Illinois to head west.

Land and homes were sold at a fraction of their value. Sacrificed for cash, the fruits of their work over five years were sold to bargain hunters and land pirates. The Camp of Israel—as the moving band of Mormons called itself—crossed the Mississippi into Iowa on February 4, 1846, and began preparations for the journey west.

Modern-day Moses

Young and other church leaders compared the Mormons' exodus from Illinois to the exodus of the children of Israel from Egypt. Young, the modern-day Moses, led his people on a journey to the Promised

The Mormons set up camps along their route as they moved westward, away from the persecution they faced at the hands of non-Mormon settlers.

Land, which took several years and covered hundreds of miles. The Mormons believed that they, like the Israelites, had left a place of persecution and were being tested along the way to prepare them for the gift of the Promised Land.

First Stop: Sugar Creek

The Mormons awoke to a freezing wind and a temperature of $-20°F$ on the morning of their departure, February 4, 1846. The street leading to the launching point on the river became known to Mormons as the Trail of Tears.[7] The first group of refugees walked

---

SOURCE DOCUMENT

THEY APPEAR TO BE GOING IN COMPANIES OF FOUR TO SIX AND TEN WAGONS, AND SOME OF THEM ARE FAIRLY WELL PROVIDED WITH TEAMS AND PROVISIONS, BUT A VERY LARGE PORTION SEEM POORLY PROVIDED FOR LONG A TRIP.

IN THE MIDST OF THIS SCENE, THE SPECTATOR CANNOT FAIL TO BE STRUCK WITH THE LIGHTNESS OF HEART, APPARENT CHEERFULNESS, AND SANGUINE HOPES WITH WHICH FAMILIES BID ADIEU TO THEIR FRIENDS, AND SET OUT ON THEIR JOURNEY. THE GREAT MASS GO FORTH, SUSTAINED AND CHEERED BY THE PROMISES OF THEIR LEADERS AND A MOST DEVOUT CONVICTION OF THE TRUTH OF THEIR RELIGION, AND THE REWARDS WHICH THEY ARE TO RECEIVE FROM HEAVEN FOR THEIR PRESENT SACRIFICE.[8]

This anonymous account of the Mormons' departure for the West appeared in the Daily Missouri Republican *in May 1846.*

down the trail and crossed the icy Mississippi by ferry, raft, and flatboat. The bitter cold did offer one advantage: The river froze, enabling families to walk across the ice into Iowa.

Arriving on the other side of the Mississippi, the Mormons traveled to Sugar Creek, ten miles west of Nauvoo, where they set up camp. There, in makeshift shelters, nine babies were born during the first few days.

On March 1, as wagons prepared to leave Sugar Creek, refugees continued to stream in, occupying shelters abandoned by those departing. Young led about a thousand Mormons five miles deeper into Iowa, where they again put up temporary housing.

As they passed through the small Iowa towns, Mormons earned money any way they could. They worked on construction projects and even sent a musical band—Captain William Pitt's brass band, made up of converts from England—to play at wakes and funerals. As quickly as scraps of lumber and iron could be salvaged or purchased, wagons were pieced together.

Six miles a day was the most the refugees could average as April rains turned much of Iowa into a deep mud puddle. The daily downpour forced them to camp for two weeks at one point and made building campfires impossible.

When the wet weather subsided, ruts carved in the earth by the water made passage difficult. The soil was warmed by the sun during the day and cooled by the chill of night, making it impossible for grass to grow.

The hungry, weakened horses slowed the pioneers' pace even more.

It was in this desperate situation that the sick, starving Mormons were rescued by what they called the miracle of the quail. Flocks of quail, tame and easy to catch, flew into their camp by the hundreds. "The sick knock them down with sticks and the little children catch them alive with their hands!" wrote Thomas Bullock, the Mormon camp recorder.[9]

Four hundred miles and four and a half months later, five hundred wagons reached Council Bluffs, Iowa, on the east bank of the Mississippi River. On the river's west bank, in Pottawatomie Indian territory, they built a way station called Winter Quarters, which served as a stop for Mormons on the journey west. Building log cabins and planting crops, they met their own needs and prepared for those who would follow.

Once set up in Winter Quarters, they backtracked and planted crops and constructed roads and bridges at strategic points along the route to ease the way for those still inching across the 120 miles of prairie.

By fall, the Mormons at Winter Quarters and Council Bluffs numbered between ten thousand and fifteen thousand. The evacuation of the City of Joseph, the name Young had given Nauvoo after Joseph Smith's death, was nearly complete.

Sailing West

The same day the Mormons started their icy trek out of Illinois—February 4, 1846—a group of about two hundred fifty other Mormons boarded a rickety ship, the *Brooklyn*, in New York Harbor and sailed for California. The ship had been chartered by Samuel Brannan, leader of the church's New York branch.

They arrived in California at the end of July. Brannan and his group established a community near present-day San Francisco. They expected that their colony, New Hope, would become headquarters for the church in the West.

Months later, Brannan took a party inland and met Young at the Green River crossing as the lead party made its way to the Great Salt Lake valley. He suggested that northern California was the place for the Mormons to settle. Young rejected Brannan's suggestion.

Samuel Brannan, leader of the church's New York branch, chartered a ship to take Mormon settlers to California.

Brannan continued with the pioneer party into the Great Salt Lake valley. However, he later returned to California on an assignment for the church and refused to return to Utah.

Mormon Battalion

The Mormons' relationship with the United States government was difficult at best. Some leaders believed that since their personal and religious liberties had not been protected by the government, the Mormons should renounce their citizenship. As they saw it, government officials had done little, if anything, over the years to stop the harassment. Smith had even approached President Martin Van Buren, seeking assistance when the Mormons were expelled from Jackson County, Missouri, but no help was offered.

However, as church leaders watched the hungry, destitute Mormons scattered all across Iowa, making their way west, they decided they would look for help wherever they could find it.

This time, politics worked in the Mormons' favor. The United States had annexed the Republic of Texas in December 1845, but the boundary between the United States and Mexico had not been clearly defined. When United States troops occupying the disputed territory along the Mexico-Texas border were attacked by the Mexican Army on May 13, 1846, Congress declared war on Mexico.

SOURCE DOCUMENT

THE EXISTING STATE OF RELATIONS BETWEEN THE UNITED STATES AND MEXICO RENDERS IT PROPER THAT I SHOULD BRING THE SUBJECT TO THE CONSIDERATION OF CONGRESS. . . .

AS WAR EXISTS, AND NOTWITHSTANDING ALL OUR EFFORTS TO AVOID IT, EXISTS BY THE ACT OF MEXICO HERSELF, WE ARE CALLED UPON BY EVERY CONSIDERATION OF DUTY AND PATRIOTISM TO VINDICATE WITH DECISION THE HONOR, RIGHTS, AND THE INTERESTS OF OUR COUNTRY. . . .

IN FURTHER VINDICATION OF OUR RIGHTS AND DEFENSE OF OUR TERRITORY, I INVOKE THE PROMPT ACTION OF CONGRESS TO RECOGNIZE THE EXISTENCE OF THE WAR, AND TO PLACE AT THE DISPOSITION OF THE EXECUTIVE THE MEANS OF PROSECUTING THE WAR WITH VIGOR, AND THUS HASTENING THE RESTORATION OF PEACE. . . .[10]

President James K. Polk, annoyed at attacks made by the Mexican Army against American troops along the Texas-Mexico border, requested a declaration of war from Congress in 1846.

Before the declaration of war, Jesse C. Little, president of one of the church's missionary branches, had contacted President James K. Polk, requesting funds to help the Mormons settle in the West. Young told Little to "take every honorable advantage of the times you can" to get aid from the federal government.[11] Young wanted to contract with the government to build forts across the country to protect the developing Oregon Trail—a route settlers were following west from the Missouri River in Missouri to the Columbia River in Oregon.

Polk originally declined the request, but after war was declared, he offered to enlist five hundred Mormons to assist in the war effort. They were to serve as soldiers in the United States Army, invading what were previously the northern provinces of Mexico and taking possession of California.

Young and most of the Mormon leaders saw the offer as a blessing. The pay and allowances offered to recruits could help buy wagons and supplies. The clothing allowance and the salaries for the unit totaled several thousand dollars, most of which would go to the soldiers' families or to the church itself.[12]

Church leaders also expected that the battalion's march west would help prepare the areas they traveled

Though President Polk declined to give financial aid to help the Mormons move west, he did offer to enlist Mormons as paid soldiers in the war against Mexico, which would provide a source of income for the church.

through for settlement. If Mormons could be the first white settlers in the area, it would free them from dealing with established settlers as they had been forced to do in Ohio, Missouri, and Illinois. In addition, their cooperation with the government helped the Mormons gain permission to camp on Indian lands and use the grass and timber.

The battalion left Winter Quarters on July 20 for Fort Leavenworth, Kansas. Their march west began in October 1846 and ended on January 29, 1847, with their arrival at the mission of San Diego in California. By July, their duty was over, and all but eighty-one (who had reenlisted) headed east to meet the Mormons on their way to the Great Salt Lake valley. Though the battalion had not engaged in any fighting while marching through present-day Arizona and New Mexico, they were instrumental in incorporating the area into the United States.

Hardship Trail

As fall faded into winter and the cattle grazed along the river bottoms, the Mormons at Winter Quarters worked diligently, building boats and rafts to get them across the river.

But preparation for the journey slowed as the Mormons' number began to diminish due to hunger, illness, and cold. The winter of 1846–1847 was insufferable for the refugees. Food and fuel disappeared. Some contracted scurvy, caused by lack of vitamin C, and some died of pulmonary diseases and cholera. Others suffered the loss of limbs from exposure to the brutal cold.

Young knew if they stayed much longer, malaria, which flourished in the river bottom, would eventually kill them all. By year's end, more than six hundred Mormons had died of disease and hunger.[13]

On January 14, 1847, Young decided that he would leave with an advance party at the first sign of spring. Their mission was to find the Promised Land in the Rocky Mountains and create a trail that other emigrants could follow.

On April 7, 1847, the Mormons were up before the sun, preparing the lead team for departure. The

Church members are gathering here for the move to the place they called their Zion.

advance party consisted of 148 pioneers (143 men, 3 women, 2 children), 93 horses, 52 mules, 66 oxen, 19 cows, 17 dogs, wagons, and numerous chickens.[14]

Once across the Elk Horn River, thirty-five miles from Winter Quarters, Young organized the party into two groups, each with a leader who would answer only to him. He also imposed a rigid code of discipline. The pioneers had to rise each morning at five and be ready to move by seven. The forward journey halted at about four each afternoon. At sunset, the wagons created a semicircle, with horses secured within the perimeter, and at eight-thirty, a bugle announced that it was time to return to the wagons for prayer. By nine, all lights were out.

Indians and Buffalo

The first scare in Indian Territory came twelve days into their trip. About 3:30 A.M., Mormon guards spotted half a dozen Pawnee Indians creeping toward camp. Sent fleeing by Mormon rifle fire, the Indians' attempt to steal horses was aborted, but the incident made the Mormons realize that they were indeed in the middle of hostile territory.

The pioneers crossed the Wood River in Nebraska in early May and worked their way along the Platte River. For the most part, they did not blaze new trails but instead used routes traveled by Indians and Oregon emigrants, as well as trails that Frémont and other explorers had described. However, they chose to travel the north bank of the Platte River—the Oregon

The Mormons blazed their own path across the United States to the West, and established a route that would be followed by many more settlers after them.

Trail followed the south bank—to avoid any chance encounters with possibly hostile Missourians who might be using the Oregon Trail.

The Platte River valley, though flat and easier to cross than the rough terrain of Iowa the year before, had its dangers. Wilford Woodruff wrote,

> Horses & cattle can walk down to [the] edge of the river & drink like walking on the edge of a smooth sea Beach, & some times while walking on the apparent hard beach or bed of the river, A man or Horse will suddenly sink into the quick sand. . . . many horses & men have been lost in this way on the Platt[e]. . . .[15]

The area along the Platte, with its wild geese and beautiful green grass, was spotted with dark piles of buffalo dung. At first, the Mormons considered the numerous deposits repugnant, but they soon discovered that the buffalo "chips" made excellent fires. The piles became important finds.

Although the pioneers welcomed the buffalo meat and were warmed by the burning dung, the huge animals also created problems. The large grazing herds left little grass for the Mormons' livestock. As Woodruff looked out at the hundreds of thousands of buffalo, he wrote, "It looked as though the face of the earth was alive & moving like the waves of the sea."[16]

William Clayton had the job of calculating the miles the pioneers had traveled by counting the revolutions of a wagon wheel. He put markers along the way for those who would follow, "From Winter

Quarters, two hundred ninety-five miles, May 8, [18]47. Camp all well. Wm. Clayton."[17]

He was relieved of the tedious counting job, however, when Orson Pratt, younger brother of Parley P. Pratt, helped Appleton Harmon make a "roadometer." Designed as an endless screw, six revolutions of a wheel turned the screw once, which then turned another wheel of sixty cogs. One mile equaled one full turn of the wheel.

As the miles passed and the Mormons moved deeper into the territory that would later become Nebraska, Indians continued to be a threat. This time it was the Sioux. Pratt wrote, "It is their custom frequently to follow emigrants hundreds of miles, keeping themselves secreted during the day, and watching the best opportunities for stealing during the night."[18]

Trading Posts and Forts

Mormons passed Fort Platte on June 1, 1847, which had been abandoned by the United States Army the previous year. Two miles farther, they reached Fort Laramie in present-day Wyoming and were greeted by James Bordeaux, the Frenchman who managed the fort. He was hospitable to the Mormons, even though he had been warned that they were thieves and that he should keep a close watch on his horses and cattle while they were in his company. The warning had come from former Missouri Governor Lilburn W. Boggs, the man who had issued the extermination order against the Mormons.

Two miles west of South Pass, in present-day Wyoming, the Mormons met Moses "Black" Harris, a mountain man, scout, and trapper, whose description of their Great Salt Lake valley destination was, "It's as barren as the back of your hand and as fertile."[19] Despite Harris's report, the Mormons pushed ahead.

On June 27, 1847—exactly three years after their prophet, Joseph Smith, and his brother Hyrum had been killed—the Mormons arrived at the Continental Divide, a ridge in the Rocky Mountains that separates rivers flowing east from those flowing west. Woodruff wrote, "I drank its waters for the first time in my life . . . I tasted of waters run[n]ing into the pacific."[20]

It had taken the Mormons four months to cross Iowa's three hundred miles and another two months to get to the Continental Divide. They were one month away from their destination, the Great Salt Lake valley.

The next day, the Mormons met Jim Bridger, a trapper headed for Fort Laramie. Young knew Bridger's reputation—few white men knew the West as well as he—and listened eagerly to Bridger's report about the Great Salt Lake valley. Bridger, who had discovered the Great Salt Lake in 1824 when he was twenty years old, talked of distances and weather, crops and water, soil and Indians. His report was more favorable than Harris's.

Final Leg of the Journey

By the end of June, the Mormons were stopped by the Green River in present-day Wyoming, which was swollen and impassable. There, they also encountered what they called "mountain fever," probably Rocky Mountain Spotted Fever, a tick-borne disease that causes nausea, vomiting, fever, and chills.[21]

On July 5, with the help of makeshift ferries, the Mormons successfully crossed the Green River. Soon, the Uinta Mountains in present-day northeastern Utah could be seen to the southwest. The Mormons' Zion lay on the other side of the mountains. They camped at Black's Fork, and, following the stream past Ham's Fork, arrived at Fort Bridger—in present-day Wyoming—on July 7, 1847.

On the road again, they took the Hastings Cutoff, crossed the Muddy Fork, and camped within a couple

Along their trip west, the Mormons met mountain man Jim Bridger. He gave them a report of the area to which they were headed.

of miles of Bear River. It was there that they met Miles Goodyear. A farmer in the Bear River valley, Goodyear had come to visit the Mormons. His favorable description of the Great Salt Lake valley sent their spirits soaring.

Their spirits dropped, however, on July 12 when Brigham Young came down with mountain fever. Falling behind with a few other wagons, he instructed the rest of the Mormons to continue. The main body moved ahead and camped at the mouth of Echo Canyon, near the present Wyoming-Utah border. The narrow valley's steep hills rose eight hundred to twelve hundred feet on both sides. The canyon was appropriately named. William Clayton wrote, "The rattling of wagons resembles carpenters hammering at boards inside the highest rocks."[22]

There, they decided that an advance party would look for the mountain pass used by the ill-fated Donner-Reed party the year before. The advance party would clear stumps and trees and prepare the narrow, difficult trail across the Wasatch Range—part of the Uinta Mountains—that would take them, and thousands of emigrants after them, into the valley below.

On July 13, the advance party found the route and proceeded to East Canyon, followed a ravine west, and crossed Big Mountain summit. Here, they locked their wheels to prevent runaway wagons and continued on the Donner-Reed trail over Little Mountain. On July 21, Orson Pratt and Erastus Snow, members of the advance party, rode down the canyon of Last Creek

The main body of travelers on the Mormon Trail camped here, at Echo Canyon, near what is now the border between Wyoming and Utah.

(later named Emigration Canyon) to the Great Salt Lake valley below and, before the sun set, planted potatoes. The next day, they dammed City Creek in the Great Salt Lake valley and brought water to the planted fields. By the fall of 1847, the torturous canyon trail would be worn smooth by the passage of hundreds of Mormons and their wagons.

By the late 1850s, the route from Iowa to Utah was so well established that travelers could purchase guidebooks from the Mormons giving distances, camping conditions, directions, and precautions for

In July 1847, the advance party would get its first view of the Great Salt Lake valley.

the entire trip. Relief wagons regularly left to meet approaching parties in Wyoming with food and fresh teams, and experienced Mormon guides escorted most groups.

After 1861, teams were sent to meet the transcontinental railroad—still under construction—at its westernmost destinations. It was not until May 10, 1869, that the railroad was completed, and emigrants could travel the entire route by train.

"This Is the Place"

On the morning of July 24, 1847, at the mouth of Emigration Canyon, Brigham Young, still sick, looked

Today, a monument bearing Young's words, "This is the place," sits at the mouth of Emigration Canyon in the Great Salt Lake valley.

over the valley before him and said, "It is enough. This is the right place, drive on."[23]

The last of the wagons had entered the valley by midafternoon. After a journey of 102 days, the Mormon advance party had finally arrived at their Promised Land.

Today, a monument sits at the mouth of Emigration Canyon, east of Salt Lake City. It is engraved with the words, "This is the place." July 24 is known as Pioneer Day and is still celebrated as a state holiday in Utah and parts of southern Idaho.

SALT LAKE CITY SAINTS

As soon as their feet touched valley soil, the Mormons started planting, irrigating, and building their new Zion. Their first winter in the valley was relatively mild, but food was scarce. In March 1848, they eagerly sowed spring seeds, but little rain fell, and the crops were damaged by late spring frosts.

Nature continued to be uncooperative when, in late May 1848, blankets of black crickets descended in swarms upon the crops. The Mormons attempted to drown them, to burn them, and to mash them, but the invading insects could not be stopped.

The harvest would have been completely lost if it had not been for what the Mormons called the miracle of the seagulls. Hundreds of birds flew in day after day from the islands in the Great Salt Lake and ate the crickets. Enough of the crops were saved by the seagulls that the Mormons were able to survive the winter. The seagull eventually became the state bird of Utah, and the cricket plague was immortalized in Mormon history as a miracle.

One year later, in 1849, the Mormons organized

the provisional State of Deseret. But United States officials did not recognize the name Deseret—a term from the Book of Mormon meaning "honeybee"—and called the new territory Utah, after the Ute Indians, who inhabited the area before the Mormons.[1]

The land the Mormons claimed as their Zion had been home to several American Indian tribes. The Ute and Shoshone nations occupied the Wasatch Range and Uinta Basin areas, and their culture was based largely on buffalo. The Hopi lived south of the Great Basin—where the advance party of the Mormons settled—and had an agricultural economy of corn, beans, squash, and small game. The nomadic Navajo and Apache herded sheep and goats and were silver workers and rug makers. The Gosiute and Paiute lived in the desert areas to the west of the Great Basin and existed on roots, berries, insects, rabbits, and antelope.

Church practice was to avoid confrontation with the Indians. Some of the Indians were converted into the church, but the majority were pushed off the land. The Mormons' relationship with the Indians in the new territory was complicated. On the one hand, they believed the Indians to be their brothers, descendants of the Lamanites of the Book of Mormon, the lost tribes of Israel. On the other hand, the Mormons' survival depended on expansion of white settlement in the Great Salt Lake valley.

In 1849, the Timpanogos Ute from Utah Valley, south of the Great Salt Lake, raided ranches in Tooele

Valley, west of Salt Lake City. The raiding party was surrounded by forty Mormon militiamen and killed.

As conflicts between the Mormons and Indians continued, smaller Mormon settlements were abandoned for the safety of larger, better-protected communities.

In July 1853 Chief Walkara (Walker), a Ute war chief, declared war on the Mormons. Known as the Walker War, the intermittent fighting dragged on for ten months before Walkara assembled his chiefs and passed the peace pipe with Brigham Young. The Mormons agreed to give the Indians whatever livestock and produce they could spare, and the Indians agreed not to attack the settlers or steal their livestock.

Federal and Territorial Conflicts

Following the discovery of gold in California in 1848, thousands of emigrants began to cross Utah on their way to the coast.

However, not all who headed west with gold fever made it to California. Many stopped along their westward journey, making the Great Salt Lake valley their home. Some were converted to the Mormon Church, but many were not.

Because of its location on one of the main thoroughfares between the Missouri River and the Pacific, Salt Lake City attracted non-Mormon merchants. Their goods and skills contributed to the growth of the Mormon city as emigrants continued to flow through the area.

Because Mormons exchanged goods and services with each other almost exclusively, and because they held all posts in the new territorial government, federal officials became concerned about the rights of non-Mormon citizens. According to Mormon historians Arrington and Bitton, "[United States President James] Buchanan and his cabinet officers found themselves in a climate of public opinion that seemed to support any move to protect the rights of non-Mormons, suppress Mormon home rule, and eradicate polygamy."[2]

President Buchanan decided to replace Brigham Young as governor of the Utah Territory. He appointed Alfred Cumming, a non-Mormon, as the new governor. Assuming the Mormons would reject a non-Mormon

SOURCE DOCUMENT

BE IT ENACTED, THAT ALL THAT PART OF THE TERRITORY OF THE UNITED STATES INCLUDED WITHIN [THE BOUNDARIES OF UTAH] . . . IS HEREBY CREATED INTO A TEMPORARY GOVERNMENT, BY THE NAME OF THE TERRITORY OF UTAH; AND, WHEN ADMITTED AS A STATE, THE SAID TERRITORY, OR ANY PORTION OF THE SAME, SHALL BE RECEIVED INTO THE UNION, WITH OR WITHOUT SLAVERY, AS THEIR CONSTITUTION MAY PRESCRIBE AT THE TIME OF THEIR ADMISSION: . . .[3]

In 1850, Congress passed the Utah Act, formally creating the territory of Utah and establishing the procedures by which Utah would eventually be admitted as a state to the Union.

governor, Buchanan suspended mail service to Utah and ordered twenty-five hundred troops to the territory in 1857 to keep the peace during the transition.

When news of the approaching troops reached the Mormons, the battles of Illinois and Missouri were still fresh in their minds. They saw Buchanan's action as open aggression against them and were determined not to be run out of their Zion again. The Utah War was launched.

Still acting as governor, Young declared martial law, reactivated the old Nauvoo Legion, and developed what he called the "scorched earth" battle plan: Grasslands were burned so the federal army's cattle would have no place to graze, and wagon trains were set on fire, destroying the army's provisions.[4] Thirty thousand Mormons evacuated their homes and headed for safety in the southern part of the Utah Territory, leaving behind only enough men to tend the crops and defend the city. Those left behind were instructed to burn the houses rather than let the army occupy them. By the fall of 1857, mountain passes were fortified with the gun power of eleven hundred Mormons.

In November 1857, Colonel Albert Sidney Johnston's troops—known as the Utah Expedition—found Fort Bridger, Wyoming, burned to the ground, as well as Fort Supply, twelve miles farther west. The troops were stopped by snowfall because of President Buchanan's decision to send them so late in the year. They fell victim to frostbite, exposure, and near starvation.

Buchanan gave Colonel Thomas L. Kane, a friend of the Mormons, permission to serve as an unofficial mediator. Kane convinced the Mormons to allow Cumming, the new governor, into the territory without a military escort. Kane brought Cumming in early April 1858. Young stepped aside, and the Mormons recognized the non-Mormon as governor.

In June 1858, Buchanan sent two representatives to the Great Salt Lake valley with a pardon for what he called Young's rebellion. Acceptance of the pardon required that the Mormons reaffirm their loyalty to the United States government. They would also have to allow a permanent army garrison to be stationed in

United States President Buchanan removed Young as governor of the Utah Territory in an effort to decrease the political power of the Mormons.

the Utah Territory in exchange for peace and amnesty. Church leaders accepted the terms of the pardon, and the families who had fled south returned to their homes in late June.

The army, under Johnston's orders, finally arrived in Utah on June 26, 1858, and established a permanent base, Camp Floyd, in Cedar Valley, west of Utah Lake. The Utah War created for the Buchanan administration an unbalanced defense budget and some political embarrassment. Johnston's army—a by-product of what some called "Buchanan's blunder"—remained in Utah for three years.[5]

Congress, concerned about the huge amount of money and manpower required to support the Utah Expedition, pressured Buchanan to bring the troops home. In addition, the national leaders' attention was being drawn away from the Mormons because of growing civil unrest over slavery. The United States also wanted the territory's help in protecting telegraph lines and overland mail from the Indians.

Mountain Meadows Massacre

Though the United States Army and the Mormons never actually fought during the Utah War—no open battles occurred and no casualties were reported—there was one catastrophic civilian confrontation.

The approach of Colonel Albert Sidney Johnston's federal army had created an atmosphere of tension among the Mormons. Trading had been halted as Mormons attempted to preserve food in preparation for what seemed like an inevitable war. This was hard on emigrant parties that had counted on purchasing supplies in Utah.

As the Fancher company—an emigrant party from Arkansas and Missouri—passed through southern Utah in August 1857 on its way to California, some of the men in the party, upset because the Mormons would not trade with them, allegedly boasted about having been involved in running the Mormons out of the Midwest.

In addition, the Indians had accused members of the Fancher party of poisoning springs and trading poisoned meat with them. As hostilities climaxed, the Mormon militia and a group of Indian allies— acting without approval of church leaders—ambushed the Fancher party. One hundred twenty men, women, and children were killed in the battle, which came to be known as the Mountain Meadows massacre.

The shock of the incident hit Mormons as hard as it did non-Mormons. Church leaders, who neither planned nor condoned the massacre, attempted to suppress the story, fearing it would feed the flames of anti-Mormon sentiment. Originally, the massacre was blamed solely on the Indians.

As details of the incident and Mormon involvement finally surfaced years later, pressure from non-Mormons and the federal government required that someone be punished. John D. Lee and Isaac Haight, Mormon leaders involved in the massacre, were excommunicated, or ousted from membership, from the church in 1870. In 1877, twenty years after the incident, Lee was sentenced by a federal court for his part in the crime and executed by a firing squad at the site of the massacre. The incident was an embarrassing one for the Salt Lake City Mormons, as they struggled to succeed in their new home.

Gold fever and the '49ers—people who went to California during the gold rush in 1849—were responsible for large numbers of emigrants settling in the American West in the mid-1800s. But there may have been no '49ers without the '48ers.

EXPANSION CONTINUES

In the spring of 1847, when James Marshall talked his boss, John Sutter, into building a sawmill at Coloma in the Sierra Nevada mountains, no one suspected that great wealth lay beneath the ground.

A year later, when it was determined that gold had been found, Henry Bigler, one of Sutter's sawmill employees, was unable to keep the discovery a secret. Bigler, a member of the Mormon Battalion, made his own search for gold, found a few particles, then unearthed a nugget. He wrote to his Mormon friends at Sutter's flour mill and urged them to come to Coloma. They also found gold nuggets, and because they had traveled "forty-six miles to look for gold, [they] became the first Forty-Eighters."[1]

On their return to the flour mill, Bigler and his companions prospected at a sandbar—later known as

SOURCE DOCUMENT

... I WENT DOWN AS USUAL, AND AFTER SHUTTING OFF THE
WATER ... , I STEPPED INTO IT, NEAR THE LOWER END, AND
THERE, UPON THE ROCK, ABOUT SIX INCHES BENEATH THE
SURFACE OF THE WATER, I DISCOVERED THE GOLD. I WAS
ENTIRELY ALONE AT THE TIME. I PICKED UP ONE OR TWO
PIECES AND EXAMINED THEM ATTENTIVELY; AND HAVING SOME
GENERAL KNOWLEDGE OF MINERALS, I COULD NOT CALL TO
MIND MORE THAN TWO WHICH ANY WAY RESEMBLED THIS—
SULPHURET OF IRON, VERY BRIGHT AND BRITTLE; AND GOLD,
BRIGHT YET MALLEABLE; I THEN TRIED IT BETWEEN TWO
ROCKS, AND FOUND THAT IT COULD BE BEATEN INTO A
DIFFERENT SHAPE, BUT NOT BROKEN. I THEN COLLECTED FOUR
OR FIVE PIECES AND WENT UP TO MR. SCOTT ... AND SAID, "I
HAVE FOUND IT."[2]

When James Marshall first found gold near Sutter's Mill, he set off the California gold rush of 1849, which would draw thousands of settlers to the West, including some to Utah.

Mormon Island—from which a fortune was eventually taken by prospectors. In August 1848, Bigler also discovered gold on the east side of the Sierra Nevada, in present-day Nevada.

Mormons Settle Nevada

In March 1849, H. S. Beatie, a Mormon on a trading expedition from Salt Lake City to California, found the east side of the Sierra Nevada so agreeable that he decided to stay. Beatie was not much interested in

Bigler's discovery of gold. Instead, he set up what would become a successful trading post.

In May 1849, more gold was found in Gold Canyon, near Beatie's trading post in Nevada County of Utah Territory, and a small community of prospectors grew.

In 1851, John Reese, a New Yorker who migrated to Utah in 1849, built what became known as Mormon Station at the western end of Carson Valley in Nevada County. He and other settlers decided they no longer wanted to be part of the Utah Territory. They met on November 12, 1852, and voted to petition Congress to create a territorial government independent of Utah. A week later, they set up the framework for that government, though they had no authority to do so.

Thomas S. Williams, a merchant-lawyer who was driving a herd of cattle to California, wrote to Brigham Young about the proposed defection: "Citizens of Carson Valley declare that they will no longer be governed by, nor tried by Mormon laws . . . declare they will pay no taxes what are levied on them from the Territory of Utah."[3]

It was not until 1862, however, that Nevada became an independent territory. In 1864, three fifths of the Utah Territory became the state of Nevada.

Mormon Corridor

Until the late 1840s, Mormon communities were established mostly in the Great Basin. Brigham Young announced in 1849 that the church would build a series of settlements between Salt Lake City and the Pacific Ocean. Known as the Mormon Corridor, the chain of ninety-eight towns would allow immigrants, who sailed from Europe around Cape Horn to California, to migrate to Salt Lake City over a land route controlled almost completely by Mormons.

A ranch, purchased by Mormons in San Bernardino, California, in 1851, blossomed to four thousand acres with fourteen hundred Mormon residents in four years. Regularly scheduled wagon lines ran between San Bernardino and Salt Lake City, stopping at settlements that sprang up along the way. San Bernardino became the second largest Mormon town by the mid-1850s.

European Converts

One hundred thirty-five more settlements were established between 1857 and 1867. From 1861 to 1868, more than twenty thousand of the settlers were converts from Europe, people the Mormons had reached with the aggressive missionary program put in place by Joseph Smith. For the most part, the converts were poor people, whose restricted lives in Europe made the possibilities of the New World attractive to them. When Brigham Young died in 1877, the population of Salt Lake City had reached one hundred forty thousand.

By 1886, forty years after the Mormons' exodus from Nauvoo on that cold February morning, one hundred thousand Mormons had crossed the continent to the Great Salt Lake valley and had become members of one of more than five hundred Mormon communities in what are now the states of Utah, Arizona, Idaho, Nevada, Colorado, Wyoming, and California.

Federal Laws

At the same time that Zion was growing in the West, concern about the Mormons was again mounting in the East. A series of bills and laws was passed by Congress to rein in the new Utah Territory, concerning the issues of separation of church and state, free enterprise, bloc voting, and polygamy.

Troubled by the fact that he could not require non-Mormon businesses to tithe—Mormons believe in paying 10 percent of their income to the church—Brigham Young initiated a boycott of businesses he considered hostile to Mormons. The boycott also included Mormon businesses that did not tithe.

At the October 1868 church conference, Young said, "I want to tell my brethren, my friends, and my enemies that we are going to draw the reins so tight as not to let a Latter-day Saint trade with an outsider."[4]

In addition to Young's boycott, the issue of polygamy continued to trouble federal lawmakers. The Republican party, which controlled Congress, decided to stop polygamy, which it often referred to as one of the "twin relics of barbarism"—the other being slavery.[5] Mormons who continued to practice polygamy were arrested following passage of the Edmunds Act

Non-Mormons were concerned about the power of the Mormons in the West. Among other tactics, non-Mormons campaigned against polygamy in an effort to decrease Mormon influence.

on March 13, 1882. Under the new law, children who were conceived in polygamous relationships before January 1, 1883, were legitimatized, and polygamists who were married before the bill were granted amnesty; but any future plural marriages were crimes, punishable by five years' imprisonment.

The Edmunds-Tucker Act of 1887 amended and strengthened the Edmunds Act. It made convicting polygamists easier, and set up an oath that residents had to take before they could vote, stating that they were not polygamists. Polygamists were also barred from jury duty. The act made funds available for federal marshals to seek out polygamists and bring them to court.

Many Mormon men went into hiding and moved from place to place to escape the marshals. Wanted posters went up and rewards were offered for the "cohabs," the pursuers' name for polygamists.[6] Between 1884 and 1893, more than a thousand judgments were secured for unlawful cohabitation and thirty-one judgments for polygamy.

The Mormons were told (though it was not contained in the Edmunds-Tucker Act) that if they abandoned polygamy, Utah would be able to acquire statehood.

The Cullom-Strubble Bill, passed in the House of Representatives in 1890, would have disenfranchised every Mormon in the Utah Territory, resulting in non-Mormons running the territorial government. It would have also deprived Mormons of their citizenship.

The majority of the Mormon male population in Utah was monogamous, having only one wife. Many of the Mormons decided they would give up their church before they would give up their citizenship. Mass defections began.[7]

In 1890, Church president Wilford Woodruff issued the Woodruff Manifesto:

> Inasmuch as laws have been enacted by Congress forbidding plural marriages, which laws have been pronounced constitutional by the court of last resort, I hereby declare my intention to submit to those laws, and to use my influence with the members of the Church over which I preside to have them do likewise.[8]

Woodruff's manifesto held up passage of the Cullom-Strubble Bill. It was eventually shelved by the Senate.

The drive for Utah statehood began again following the manifesto. In January 1896, Utah was admitted to the Union as the forty-fifth state, the Beehive State. Mormons in the new state were a quarter of a million strong and had constructed four temples in the cities of St. George, Logan, Manti, and Salt Lake City.

B eliving the land was theirs, given to them by God, the Mormons clung to the words Joseph Smith had said a few months before he was killed: "The whole of America is Zion itself from north to south."[1]

THE LEGACY

The Mormons proceeded to build a religion that would attract millions of members from all over the world.

When the Mormons of Utah celebrated the centennial of their 1847 arrival in the Great Salt Lake valley, church membership exceeded the one million mark.

By the 1950s, Mormons had gone from "vilified" to "venerated" and from obscurity to one of the largest Christian churches in the United States.[2] Today, it is one of the fastest-growing religions in the world. The first temples outside the United States were built during the early part of the twentieth century in Canada and pre-statehood Hawaii.

By the early 1970s, the church had more than 3 million members. The growth can be attributed, in part, to a vigorous missionary program. Missionaries—young men and women between the ages of nineteen and twenty-six—are sent to 160 nations and territories around the world to serve one-and-a-half- to two-year unpaid missions.

Though men were missionaries from the earliest years of the church, women were not sent on missions until 1898. Of the more than fifty thousand full-time missionaries, far more—75 percent—are still male than female.

Priesthood

It was in the late 1970s that the church's position on people of African lineage and the priesthood changed. People of African descent were allowed to join the church from the beginning, but before 1978, males of African descent were not allowed to hold the priest-hood—a position open to other worthy males. Only members of the priesthood can perform rites such as baptism, confirmation, and blessing and passing the sacrament (communion).

On June 9, 1978, Church president Spencer W. Kimball said that it was revealed to him (Mormons believe God speaks to present-day prophets) that eligibility for the priesthood should be available to worthy males of all races. Women, however, are still excluded from holding the priesthood.

Trail of Hope

To commemorate the one hundred fiftieth anniversary of the Mormon Trail, a group of Mormons reenacted the pioneers' trek to Utah. They left Omaha, Nebraska (the original Winter Quarters), on April 21, 1997, and followed the path that many of their ancestors had traveled.

On May 23, they camped in Keystone, Nebraska, a town with a population of sixty. "We literally tripled the population of the town," Joseph Johnstun of Salt Lake City said.[3]

Some days as many as eight hundred people—both Mormons and non-Mormons—walked part of the memorable ninety-three-day journey. Thirty horse-drawn covered wagons and a dozen handcarts completed the reenactment company. "We're getting to places we recognize—places we've heard about all our lives," Johnstun said on May 29, 1997.[4]

They were greeted with cheers, bands, and celebrations on their arrival in Salt Lake City in July 1997—one hundred fifty years after the original pioneers entered the valley.

Mormons Today

In the 1980s, a quarter of a million new members were added to the ranks each year. By 1982, membership passed the 5 million mark. Of the church's 10 million members in the late 1990s, just over 50 percent resided outside the United States. Alberta, Canada; London, England; Berne, Switzerland; Hamilton, New Zealand; Mexico City, Mexico; Tokyo, Japan; Mapusaga, American Samoa; and São Paulo, Brazil, are major centers of Mormonism outside the United States.

Utah now has 2 million residents. The Great Salt Lake valley—Salt Lake City and the surrounding communities—is home to more than a million people. Temple Square, in the heart of Salt Lake City, holds a temple, visitors' centers, authentic pioneer cabin, and Tabernacle, which houses one of the world's largest pipe organs. The Tabernacle is also home to the world-famous Mormon Tabernacle Choir, a 325-voice group that was organized shortly after the Mormons arrived in Utah in 1847. The choir has been featured on *Music and the Spoken Word*, a radio program that has been broadcast around the world since 1929.

Growing out of proportion to other religions, the church has assets estimated at $30 billion, according to *Time* magazine.[5] (Church president Gordon B. Hinckley has claimed the figure was exaggerated.) No major United States religion is as rich or as economically active.

Church leaders invest most of the donations and tithes in church-owned, for-profit concerns. The church owns banks, newspapers, retail stores, radio stations, a television studio, and life insurance companies, along with other investments. The growth of the church's membership is so rapid that a reorganization of middle management was announced in April 1997 by Church president Hinckley.

Eighty-eight million copies of the Book of Mormon have been published since 1830. The book has been printed in forty languages, and selections from it have been printed in an additional forty-eight

The Salt Lake City Temple stands at the heart of Temple Square in present-day Salt Lake City, reminding observers of the success of the Mormons and their continuing growth and expansion.

languages. Mormons base their faith on this book along with the Doctrine and Covenants, which contains revelations given to Joseph Smith, and the Pearl of Great Price, an additional selection of Smith's revelations, translations, and narrations.

Mormons in American History

The Mormons were significant players in the settlement of the American West. Brigham Young and the original Mormon pioneers to Utah, Samuel Brannan and the Mormons aboard the *Brooklyn*, the Mormon Battalion, and European converts helped populate the towns that made up the early West.

A street in present-day San Francisco is named after Brannan. His books, shipped in crates on the *Brooklyn*, were kept in what later became California's first library in San Francisco. That city's first bank, express, and shipping businesses were established by Mormons. Mormons started the first post office in the village of Brooklyn, which is present-day Oakland, California.

The Mormons were instrumental in the completion of the transcontinental railroad, the development of the overland mail, and the explosion of the California gold rush. Their religion began with the prayers of a fourteen-year-old boy who was confused over which church he should join. That boy, Joseph Smith, founded what became one of the fastest-growing religions in the world.

★ TIMELINE ★

1805—*December 23*: Joseph Smith, Jr., born.

1820—*Spring*: Smith reports his first vision.

1823—*September 21–22*: Smith reports a visitation from the angel Moroni.

1825—*October*: Smith lives in Isaac Hale's home.

1826—*March 20*: Smith is tried and convicted for being disorderly and an impostor.

1827—*January 18*: Smith marries Emma Hale.
September 22: Smith reports taking the golden plates from the hill Cumorah.
December: Joseph and Emma Smith move to Harmony, Pennsylvania.

1828—*April*: Martin Harris becomes a scribe for Smith.

1829—*April 7*: Oliver Cowdery replaces Martin Harris as scribe.
July: Translation of the Book of Mormon completed; Smith performs first baptisms.

1830—*March*: The Book of Mormon first published.
April 6: Church of Jesus Christ organized.

1831—*January*: Joseph and Emma Smith move to Kirtland, Ohio.
July: Smith names site for City of Zion in Missouri.
September 2: Joseph and Emma Smith move to Hiram, Ohio.

1832—*April 1*: Smith visits settlements in Missouri; Emma Smith moves to Kirtland.
June: Smith joins Emma in Kirtland.

1833—*February 27*: Smith records the Word of Wisdom.
July: Smith helps lay cornerstone for Kirtland Temple; Mormons agree to leave Jackson County, Missouri.

1834—*May 3*: Church name changed to Church of the Latter-day Saints.

1836—*March 27*: Temple in Kirtland, Ohio, dedicated.

1838—*January 12*: Smith leaves Kirtland for Far West, Missouri.
April 23: Church name changed to the Church of Jesus Christ of Latter-day Saints.
June: Danites organized.
August 6: Mormons fight non-Mormons at Gallatin, Missouri.
October 27: Missouri Governor Lilburn Boggs issues order to exterminate Mormons.
October 31: Smith surrenders at Far West and is imprisoned.
November: Smith attends Richmond hearing.
December 1: Smith awaits trial in Liberty Jail.

1839—*April 15–16*: Smith escapes while being taken to Boone County for change of venue.
May 10: Smith moves with his family to Illinois.

1840—*December 16*: Nauvoo city charter becomes law.

1841—*April 6*: Smith lays cornerstone for Nauvoo Temple.

1842—*Summer*: Rumors of polygamy circulate.

1843—*July 12*: Smith secretly records revelation on celestial marriage (polygamy).

1844—*January 29*: Smith announces his candidacy for president of the United States.
February 20: Smith instructs Twelve Apostles to investigate Oregon and California for possible relocation.
June 7: Mormon dissidents publish first and only issue of the *Nauvoo Expositor* newspaper.
June 10: Smith orders destruction of the rival newspaper's press.
June 12: Smith and his brother Hyrum arrested for destroying press and charged with treason.
June 18: Smith places Nauvoo under martial law.
June 24: Joseph and Hyrum Smith surrender and are taken to jail in Carthage, Illinois.
June 27: Joseph and Hyrum Smith killed by a mob in Carthage Jail.
August: Brigham Young voted new prophet and president of the church.

1845—*January*: Illinois state legislature repeals Nauvoo's charter.
May 19: Defendants found not guilty of murder in the deaths of Joseph and Hyrum Smith.
October 1: Brigham Young announces that the Mormons will leave Illinois for the West.

1846—*February 4*: Mormons leave Illinois, crossing the Mississippi River into Iowa.

July 20: Mormon Battalion leaves Winter Quarters, Nebraska, for Fort Leavenworth, Kansas.

Fall: Mormons relocate at Winter Quarters; Evacuation of Nauvoo completed.

1847—*April*: Advance party of 148 pioneers departs into Indian Territory.

July 24: Young and the last of the wagons making up the advance party arrive in the Great Salt Lake valley.

1849—Utah Territory established.

1853—*July*: Ute war chief Walkara (Walker) declares war on the Mormons.

1857—Utah War waged when federal government sends Utah Expedition to rid the state of polygamy and protect non-Mormons' rights.

September: Mormons and Indians kill more than one hundred emigrants in Mountain Meadows massacre.

1877—*August 29*: Brigham Young dies.

1887—Congress passes Edmunds-Tucker Act.

June: Polygamy becomes illegal in Utah Territory.

1896—Utah becomes a state.

1947—Church membership exceeds one million mark.

1978—*June*: Priesthood extended to males of African lineage.

1982—Church has more than 5 million members.

1997—Church president Gordon B. Hinckley announces reorganization to manage rapid growth.
April 21: Group of Mormons reenacts the pioneers' trek to Utah.

★ CHAPTER NOTES ★

Chapter 1. The Vision of a Teenage Boy

1. Fawn M. Brodie, *No Man Knows My History: The Life of Joseph Smith*, 2nd ed. (New York: Vintage Books, 1995), p. 17.

2. Lucy Smith, *Biographical Sketches of Joseph Smith the Prophet, and His Progenitors for Many Generations* (Liverpool: Published for Orson Pratt by S. W. Richards, 1853), p. 82.

Chapter 2. A Church Is Formed

1. Lucy Smith, *Biographical Sketches of Joseph Smith the Prophet, and His Progenitors for Many Generations* (Liverpool: Published for Orson Pratt by S. W. Richards, 1853), pp. 50–51.

2. Fawn M. Brodie, *No Man Knows My History: The Life of Joseph Smith*, 2nd ed. (New York: Vintage Books, 1995), p. 18.

3. Leonard J. Arrington and Davis Bitton, *The Mormon Experience: A History of the Latter-day Saints*, 2nd ed. (Urbana: University of Illinois Press, 1992), p. 9.

4. Smith, pp. 91–92.

5. Brodie, p. 29.

6. Ibid., p. 433.

7. "The Words of Mormon," *The Book of Mormon* (Salt Lake City: The Church of Jesus Christ of Latter-day Saints, 1952), p. 132.

8. Brodie, pp. 42–43.

9. B. H. Roberts, *Outlines of Ecclesiastical History: A Text Book* (Salt Lake City: Deseret Book Company, 1979), p. 306.

10. *The Book of Mormon* (Salt Lake City: The Church of Jesus Christ of Latter-day Saints, 1952), n.p.

Chapter 3. Latter-day Saints' Beliefs

1. Joseph Smith, *The Pearl of Great Price* (Salt Lake City: The Church of Jesus Christ of Latter-day Saints, 1952), p. 59.

2. B. H. Roberts, *Outlines of Ecclesiastical History: A Text Book* (Salt Lake City: Deseret Book Company, 1979), p. 424.

3. Leonard J. Arrington and Davis Bitton, *The Mormon Experience: A History of the Latter-day Saints*, 2nd ed. (Urbana: University of Illinois Press, 1992), p. 299.

4. Thomas F. O'Dea, *The Mormons*, Phoenix ed. (Chicago: The University of Chicago Press, 1964), p. 60.

5. Arrington and Bitton, p. 55.

Chapter 4. Gentiles versus Saints

1. Harold Schindler, *Orrin Porter Rockwell: Man of God, Son of Thunder*, 2nd ed. (Salt Lake City: University of Utah Press, 1983), p. 11.

2. Fawn M. Brodie, *No Man Knows My History: The Life of Joseph Smith*, 2nd ed. (New York: Vintage Books, 1995), p. 225.

3. Ibid., pp. 234–235.

4. Schindler, p. 54.

5. Ibid., p. 56.

Chapter 5. The City of Joseph

1. Huston Horn, *The Old West: The Pioneers* (New York: Time-Life Books, 1974), p. 167.

2. Thomas F. O'Dea, *The Mormons*, Phoenix ed. (Chicago: University of Chicago Press, 1964), p. 50.

3. Harold Schindler, *Orrin Porter Rockwell: Man of God, Son of Thunder*, 2nd ed. (Salt Lake City: University of Utah Press, 1983), pp. 113–114.

4. Ibid., p. 71.

5. Fawn M. Brodie, *No Man Knows My History: The Life of Joseph Smith*, 2nd ed. (New York: Vintage Books, 1995), p. 383.

6. Joseph Smith, *The Doctrine and Covenants of the Church of Jesus Christ of Latter-day Saints* (Salt Lake City: The Church of Jesus Christ of Latter-day Saints, 1971), 135:4, p. 487.

7. Schindler, p. 124.

8. Brodie, p. 393.

9. Ibid., p. 394.

10. Schindler, p. 126.

11. Ibid.

Chapter 6. Final Exodus

1. Thomas F. O'Dea, *The Mormons*, Phoenix ed. (Chicago: University of Chicago Press, 1964), pp. 77–78.

2. Fawn M. Brodie, *No Man Knows My History: The Life of Joseph Smith*, 2nd ed. (New York: Vintage Books, 1995), p. 162.

3. B. H. Roberts, *Outlines of Ecclesiastical History: A Text Book* (Salt Lake City: Deseret Book Company, 1979), p. 432.

4. Leonard J. Arrington and Davis Bitton, *The Mormon Experience: A History of the Latter-day Saints*, 2nd ed. (Urbana: University of Illinois Press, 1992), p. 84.

5. Ibid., p. 94.

6. O'Dea, p. 73.

7. Maurine Jensen Proctor and Scot Facer Proctor, *The Gathering: Mormon Pioneers on the Trail to Zion* (Salt Lake City: Deseret Book Company, 1996), p. 65.

8. In David Colbert, ed., *Eyewitness to America: 500 Years of America in the Words of Those Who Saw It Happen* (New York: Pantheon Books, 1997), p. 166.

9. Proctor and Proctor, p. 106.

10. In Henry Steele Commager, ed., *Documents of American History* (New York: Appleton-Century-Crofts, Inc., 1958), vol. 1, pp. 310–311.

11. Arrington and Bitton, p. 98.

12. Ibid., p. 99.

13. Huston Horn, *The Old West: The Pioneers* (New York: Time-Life Books, 1974), p. 170.

14. O'Dea, p. 80.

15. Scott G. Kenney, ed., *Wilford Woodruff's Journal, 1833–1898*, (Midvale, Utah: Signature Books, 1983), vol. 3, p. 151.

16. Ibid., p. 171.

17. Proctor and Proctor, pp. 124–126.

18. Ibid., p. 129.

19. Harold Schindler, *Orrin Porter Rockwell: Man of God, Son of Thunder*, 2nd ed. (Salt Lake City: University of Utah Press, 1983), p. 160.

20. Kenney, p. 219.

21. Thomas G. Alexander, *Utah, The Right Place: The Official Centennial History* (Salt Lake City: Gibbs-Smith Publisher, 1995), p. 94.

22. *William Clayton's Journal* (Dallas: L. K. Taylor Publishing Company, 1973), p. 296.

23. O'Dea, p. 82.

Chapter 7. Salt Lake City Saints

1. Joseph Smith, Jr., trans., *The Book of Mormon* (Salt Lake City: The Church of Jesus Christ of Latter-day Saints, 1952), p. 480.

2. Leonard J. Arrington and Davis Bitton, *The Mormon Experience: A History of the Latter-day Saints*, 2nd ed. (Urbana: University of Illinois Press, 1992), p. 166.

3. In Henry Steele Commager, ed., *Documents of American History* (New York: Appleton-Century-Crofts, Inc., 1958), vol. 1, p. 321.

4. Arrington and Bitton, p. 166.

5. James B. Allen and Glen M. Leonard, *The Story of the Latter-day Saints* (Salt Lake City: Deseret Book Company, 1976), p. 309.

Chapter 8. Expansion Continues

1. Irving Stone, *Men to Match My Mountains: The Opening of the Far West, 1840–1900* (New York: Berkley Books, 1956), p. 134.

2. In David Colbert, ed., *Eyewitness to America: 500 Years of America in the Words of Those Who Saw It Happen* (New York: Pantheon Books, 1997), p. 171.

3. Stone, p. 211.

4. Ibid., p. 332.

5. James B. Allen and Glen M. Leonard, *The Story of the Latter-day Saints* (Salt Lake City: Deseret Book Company, 1976), p. 291.

6. Ibid., p. 396.

7. Stone, p. 509.

8. Joseph Smith, Jr., *The Doctrine and Covenants of the Church of Jesus Christ of Latter-day Saints* (Salt Lake City: The Church of Jesus Christ of Latter-day Saints, 1952), p. 257.

Chapter 9. The Legacy

1. Thomas F. O'Dea, *The Mormons*, Phoenix ed. (Chicago: University of Chicago Press, 1964), p. 171.

2. David Van Biema, "Kingdom Come," *Time*, August 4, 1997, p. 52.

3. "Re-Enactment Trek," *The Salt Lake Tribune*, May 23, 1997, p. A2.

4. "Re-Enactment Trek," *The Salt Lake Tribune*, May 29, 1997, p. A2.

5. Van Biema, p. 52.

★ FURTHER READING ★

Books

Arrington, Leonard J., and Davis Bitton. *The Mormon Experience: A History of the Latter-day Saints.* Urbana: University of Illinois Press, 1992.

Brodie, Fawn M. *No Man Knows My History: The Life of Joseph Smith.* New York: Vintage Books, 1995.

Perrone, Vito. *Joseph Smith.* New York: Chelsea House, 1995.

Sanford, William R., and Carl R. Green. *Brigham Young: Pioneer and Mormon Leader.* Springfield, N.J.: Enslow Publishers, Inc., 1996.

Simon, Charnan. *Brigham Young: Mormon & Pioneer.* Danbury, Conn.: Children's Press, 1998.

Williams, Jean K. *The Mormons.* Danbury, Conn.: Franklin Watts, 1996.

Internet Addresses

Bertola, Max. *The Mormon Pioneer Story.* 1995. <http://www.uvol.com/pioneer/homepage.html> (August 26, 1998).

Public Broadcasting System. *Trail of Hope: The Story of the Mormon Trail.* 1997. <http://www.pbs.org/trailofhope> (August 26, 1998).

★ INDEX ★